Economic History of Early Medieval Northern India

Economic History of Early Medieval Northern India

Gian Chand Chauhan

ATLANTIC
PUBLISHERS & DISTRIBUTORS

Published by
ATLANTIC PUBLISHERS AND DISTRIBUTORS
B-2, Vishal Enclave, Opp. Rajouri Garden, New Delhi-27
Phones : 25413460, 25429987, 25466842

Sales Office
7/22, Ansari Road, Darya Ganj, New Delhi-02
Phones : 23273880, 23285873, 23280451
Fax : 91-11-23285873
web : www.atlanticbooks.com
e-mail : info@atlanticbooks.com

ISBN 81-269-0260-4

Typeset at
APD Computer Graphics, Delhi
Printed in India at
Nice Printing Press, Delhi

Dedicated to My Kulaīṣṭa

Śri Doom Śaṛitā Nagarkoṭiyā

Ya Devā Sarva Bhūteṣu
Chetenya Bhidhīyate Namastasiya
Namastaisya, Namastaisya Namo Namaḥ

Preface

The serious research of the early medieval Northern India began in the second half of the 20th century and with it came acute ideological debates over the nature of the "historical quarry", from which not only historians, but philosophers, sociologists and anthropologists took the material for constructing their theoretical postulates. The early medieval Indian history attracted the attention of specialists and historians. The Harṣa Empire lasted for some thirty years. After his death it fell apart and for the following few centuries India was fragmented into numerous small states which were continually fighting among themselves, making temporary alliances and once again fighting with one another.

The *Economic History of Early Medieval Northern India* (from C. 8th to 1000 A.D.) is an attempt to present the picture of the agricultural development and economic changing which early Medieval Northern India has experienced. The present book aims at presenting a comprehensive and systematic study of one of the economic institutions entitled "Agrarian Formation and Feudal Economy" dealing with the various aspects such as agriculture, types of crops, nature of peasantry, its different interpretations, land-grant, its impact on early Medieval economy, internal and external trade, urban concept; forced labour and paucity of coins etc. I have restricted my study C. 8th to 1000 A.D. This study has been based on the archaeological and literary sources.

In the chapters that follow I intend to deal with the Economic History of Early Medieval Northern India. It would be impossible in a sketch as brief as this to give even superficial account of the characteristics of Agrarian and Economic History of Early Medieval Northern India. But the reader would be better prepared to understand the features of such a society if he or she first grasped the importance of certain developments and changes which took place in early medieval history. I shall deal fully with early medieval India and scarcely at all with Northern India. Due to limitations of space and time, I shall be mainly confined to the 8th, 9th and 10th centuries.

The book has been divided into six chapters. The first chapter deals with the sketchy reviews of some of the valuable publications. Moreover, the learned authors have explored various sources available at present, but still important topics such as agricultural development, nature of peasantry, land-grants and its impact on early Medieval Economy etc., are to be taken afresh. The second chapter discusses various features of early medieval economy in Northern India such as paucity of coins, urban decay, dependent peasantry, rot in external and internal trades.

The third chapter concerns with the nature of early medieval peasantry and its impact on early medieval economy. The term "peasantry" is one which may have different meanings and interpretations. Even if we ignore its various meanings and interpretations, there exist many attempts as its analysis and definition which do not seem to be very closely related to one another. But if we limit ourselves to essentials and are prepared to overlook the subtle nuances of meaning which scholars and particularly historians do. Hence, the term is used by historians into various distinct senses.

The fourth chapter deals with the nature of land-grants and its impact on early medieval economy. More and more land was granted out in holding, and those who received this land acquired greater rights in relation to both the control powers and the population dependent upon them. The overwhelming majority of the charters that have come down to us from 8th to 10th centuries tell of such gifts bestowed upon *Brāhmaṇa,* Buddhist monks and religious establishments. A few documents registering the granting of land holdings to lay persons have also been preserved and these are of the same type as those granting to the *Brāhmaṇas*.

The fifth chapter concerns with the agricultural developments which is an important ingredient of the economic life of the people in early medieval Northern India. Early Medieval India being an agricultural state, it is the mainstay of the people. As a picture has been depicted of features of the agrarian economy like agricultural castes, classification of soil for the purpose of raising crops of different kinds, methods employed in cultivations, agricultural implements, agricultural seasons for sowing and harvesting, different kinds of crops produced etc. The conclusion emerging from this long labour of love constitute the sixth and the last chapter.

The present book necessarily owes much to the works of scholars who have studied or are studying the economic and agrarian institutions of early medieval India, but some of the ideas put forward are my own and derived from my independent research. Since my aim is to place at the disposal of the educated people a general outline of one of the great economic institution of early medieval Indian history, as it appears in the light of most recent research. I have refrained from elaborate and controversial annotation. A brief bibliography is given for the benefit of the scholars who desire to push his research further. I express my deep gratitude to my esteemed teacher, Prof. J.K. Sharma, whose constant guidance made it possible for me to complete this book. I do not have enough words to express what I owe to my father B.R. Chauhan for his constant encouragement and good wishes for the accomplishment of this book. My thanks are due to Mrs. Shakila Chauhan, M.A. (Sanskrit & Fine Art) who rendered most valuable assistance in translating many Sanskrit passages into Hindi. I shall be failing in my duty if do not acknowledge my indebtedness to Indian Council of Historical Research [ICHR] whose scholarship I enjoyed during 1997-99.

GIAN CHAND CHAUHAN

Contents

ABBREVIATIONS

ABORI	Annals of the Bhandarkar Oriental Research Institute, Poona.
Āit. Bṛ	Āitareya Brāhmaṇa
Agn. P.	Agni-Purāṇa
A.I.	Ancient India
Aś	Arthashāstra of Kauṭilya
B.O.R.I.	Bhandarkar Oriental Research Institute.
Bhag. P.	Bhāgvata Purāṇa
Brāh. P.	Brāhmaṇda Purāṇa
Bṛ. S.	Bṛhaspati, Smṛti
C.I.I.	Corpus Inscriptionum Indicarum Various Volumes.
C.P.	Copper-Plates.
E.I.	*Epigraphia Indica*, Calcutta and Delhi, Various Volumes.
IESHR	Indian Economic and Social History Review.
H.C.	Harṣacarita (tr.) by Cowell.
H.E.S.A.	Harshachrita — Ek-Sānskritik Adhayan V.S. Agarwal, Patna.
I.A.	Indian Antiquary, Bombay.
I.F.	Indian Feudalism, R.S. Sharma.
P.I.H.C.	Proceeding of Indian History Congress.
I.H.Q.	Indian Historical Quarterly, Calcutta.
J.A.O.S.	Journal of American Oriental Society, Baltimore.
J.A.S.B.	Journal of Asiatic Society of Bengal, Calcutta.
Jāt	Jātakas
J.B.B.R.A.S.	Journal of the Bombay Branch of the Royal Asiatic Society, Bombay.

J.B.O.R.S.	Journal of the Bihar and Orissa Research Society, Patna.
J.B.R.S.	Journal of the Bihar Research Society, Patna.
J.E.S.H.O.	Journal of the Economic and Social History of the Orient, Leiden.
J.G.R.I.	Journal of the Ganga Nath Jha Research Institute, Allahabad.
J.I.H.	Journal of the Indian History, Trivandrum.
J.N.S.I.	Journal of the Numismatic Society of India, Allahabad.
J.O.R.	Journal of the Oriental Research, Madras.
J.R. A.S.	Journal of the Royal Asiatic Society of Great Britain and Ireland, London.
Kātha. S.	Kathāsaritsāgara.
Kāma. S.	Kāmasūtra of Vatasayāna.
Kātya. S.	Kātyāna Smṛti
LSRSEI	Land System and Rural Society in India.
Manu	Manu Smṛti
Māt. P.	Mātsya Purāṇa
Mbh.	Mahābhārata
Nār. S.	Nārada Smṛti
Rāj	Rājatarangaṇi of Kalhaṇa (tr.) M.A. Stein.
Rāmā.	Rāmāyaṇa
S.B.B.	Sacred Books of the Buddhist.
S.B.E.	Sacred Books of the East.
Śat. Br.	Śātapatha Brāhmaṇa
S.I.	Select Inscription, Vol. I and II, D.C. Sircar.
SI. Yu-ki	Buddhist Records of the Western World by S. Beal.
Skanda P.	Skanḍa Purāṇa
Viṣṇu P.	Viṣṇu Purāṇa.
Viṣṇu S.	Viṣṇu Smṛti
Yājñ. S.	Yājñavalkya Smṛti

Roman Equivalents of Nāgarī Letters

अ a	आ ā	इ I	ई ī	
उ u	ऊ Ū	ऋ Ṛ	ए E	
ऐ Ai	ओ O	औ au		
क K	ख kh	ग G	घ GH	
ङ N	च C	छ CH	ज J	
झ Jh	न n	ट Ṭ	ठ Ṭh	
ड Ḍ	ढ ḌH	ण Ṇ	त T	
थ TH	द D	ध् DH	न् N	
प P	फ PH	ब B	भ BH	
म M	य Y	र R	ल L	
व V	श Ś	ष ṣ	स S	ह H
क्ष ksh	श्र Ṭra	ज्ञ GHY		

Anusvara: Ṃ　　Visarga : ḥ

1

Writing on Economy of Early Medieval Northern India: A Historiographical Critique

The term "agrarian" seems to be used in a way by modern social scientists, just to describe all socio-economic structures, policies, programmes, problems, public measures and law which have to do with distribution and tenure of farm or agricultural land and with the social, economic, and political status of those either lives on agricultural land or are dependent on agriculture for a livelihood.

The present work is an attempt to make an evolution of one of the most critical period of the Indian history with main focus on Economic structure. It is usually asserted that the people of Ancient India fell easy prey to the conquerors. This might have because of the peasantry of the ancient India, which constituted more than ninety per cent of total population. It is said that they were so heavily exploited that they passively accepted almost any conquest expecting it to bring a change for the better. The character and role of peasantry in early India is a complex and poorly investigated problem, due to the scarcity of sources and insufficient attention given to it by the scholars. Many of the agrarian aspects have so far remained obscure including the status and role of the peasantry. The continual change in state borders or geographical maps went on changing for several centuries. At the same time both feudal agrarian relation and system of social-economic and feudal elements in culture got changed. Early Indian inscriptions indicate that land grant grew considerably, and through them we are able to trace the development and changes in feudal agrarian structure. Documents of early India's listing an increasingly larger number of taxes exacted from the peoples, the formation of immunity *i.e.*, the prohibition to trespasses of granted territory, the loss of state control over donated land and weakening of state power; and more frequently the peasants found themselves in increasing feudal dependence.

The present work intends to trace the evolution of early Indian economic structure chiefly between the period from eight century A.D., and concludes with the Turkish raids in northern India in the tenth century A.D., which in turn inaugurated the Medieval period which covered at the best fragmentarily in the existing socio-economic literature. It marks the coming of new institution which strengthened the feudal element, and this period too marks the zenith of ancient Indian feudal system. Its beginning synchronises with the disintegration of empires. This was a period of political fragmentations with state formation continually replacing each other. It was a time when one locality might at one time be the centre of a small principality, at another have its power extended over a more longer area and again break up, became part of another empire.

However, during this period, we notice certain new developments and changes in polity, economic, social organisation, religion and culture. It seems that feudalism touched every aspects of life and it caused disintegration at all levels. The value based democratic concept of earlier phase was over. The society become class, caste and creed-based. The concept of nationalism narrowed down and the concept of regionalism developed. Feudal structure was giving rise to political disunity, division and sub-divisions. Each small unit was becoming an isolated one. Economy, polity, society, religion, and art and architecture began to develop separately for each unit. Various orthodox were born due to development of the caste and untouchability and thus social disintegration. Medievalism developed at all levels giving birth to taboos, orthodoxy, rigidity of belief and thinking. This period of Indian history saw the rise and the flourishing stage of feudal system, and reflects the history of bitter feudal conflict between the peasants and feudal lords? It not only throw some light on ignorance, religious fanaticism, and feudal brutality but also throw light on economic structure and feudal economy.

The study of the socio-economic formation of early India is currently engaging the attention of the scholars of the ancient Indian history. It continues to baffle the scholars. There have been many valuable publications in past which present the economic life and feudal agrarian structure in ancient India. Agrarian formation has found mentioned as a chapter or article in many works dealing with the socio-economic formation in Indian history, taking into account one or the other portion of the period under analyses. However, the credit goes to U.N. Ghoshal, who for the first time ventured to explore the myth of agrarian relation in India, with a limited sources to which he has frankly mentioned in his monograph, *The Agrarian System in Ancient India,*[1] Calcutta, 1929-30. It is undoubtedly one of the most considerable contribution made to this interesting topic. The author's information is extensive. But with the coming of Archaeology, a flood of information has come out, which reveals that the agrarian structure and its characters were undergoing change. The condition and situation was not alike throughout ancient Indian history. His another work, *Contribution to the History of Hindu Revenue System,* Calcutta, 1940[2], is a valuable contribution to the economic history of ancient and Medieval India. It discusses the growth of agriculture and land revenue system in Indian history. The growth of agriculture and trade led to the formation of wealthy land-owing classes and rich trading communities. However, the introduction of iron for the purpose of agricultural production. This might have strengthened the economic condition of land owners. With the increasing emphasis on agriculture, more labourers were needed for cultivation of land. This might be a motivating factor to employ slave for agricultural production. B.N. Datta has assigned a full chapter on feudal structure in his work, *Dialectics of Land Economics in India,*[3] Calcutta, 1952. But the best representative of the Marxist historiography in India is D.D. Kosambi, the father of Indian feudalism. His work, *An Introduction to the Study of Indian History*[4], Bombay, 1956 which surveys the course of Indian history right from the earliest time to till the British Conquest, and throws much light on feudal system in Indian history. He has also contributed many papers on feudalism in various journals.

But he does not show any proliferate an adherence to slavery, in Indian history. He is of the opinion that slaves in ancient India were specially house slaves and completely denied the slave mode of production, but his theory is questioned by D.R. Chanana, *Slavery in Ancient India,*[5] Delhi, 1960, is a major contribution to over knowledge of the origin, extent and nature of slavery in ancient India.

However, Kosambi's attempts to distinguish two processes in development of feudalism in ancient Indian history, that is "feudalism from above", and "feudalism from below". When the kings began to transfer their administrative rights to their subordinates chiefs who thus came into direct relation with pleasantry — a process he calls, "feudalism from above". It reached an advanced stage of development during Gupta and post Gupta's periods, "a class of land owner developed within the village between the state and the peasantry, gradually to wield armed power on the local population" — a process he terms, "feudalism from below".[6] A direct influence of Marxist ideology is also seen in the writing of Kosambi's; generally his works give an idea of changes in early Indian society and economy. P. Niyogi's *Contribution to the Economic History of Northern India, From the Tenth to the Twelfth Century A.D.*[7], Calcutta, 1962, it can legitimately claim to be the first of its kind to dealing with the outstanding features of a period. She has discussed in detail about land, land measurement, trade and commerce, crafts currency, state income and expenditure. Her study throws much light on the general pattern of the economic system, which spread over a vast area, was resulted in the study of economic history of ancient India. However, her work does not cover the whole span of our period. Moreover the learned scholars has left out the discussion of a most important topic like peasant condition and economic impact on social institution. B.N. Ganguli, edited work, *Reading in Indian Economic History,*[8] Delhi, 1964. The work is simply a collection of articles lays stress on those aspects of the economic history which have been received scholarly attention, some changes have been introduced to the original. The edited articles have been presented in the first all India seminar on Indian economic history, in Delhi School of Economic. We notice that general idea of changes in

Ancient Indian Economy have been depicted in these articles. L. Gopal, in his works *Economic Life of North India*[9] A.D. 700-1200, Delhi 1965 (Rev. 1989), *Aspects of The History of Agriculture in Ancient India*,[10] Varanasi, 1980, discusses the various approaches and techniques to the agriculture in ancient and early medieval Indian agricultural history. It is difficult to establish a definite co-relationship between production and feudal rent. He suggests the private ownership in agricultural land. He further states that the state had proprietary right over certain fields; received revenue from the peasants as the wages for the protection is afforded to the people, and he further assumes that agricultural land generally belonged to him who cultivated it. His statement seems to be contradictory. He throws much light particularly on the emergence of feudalism in Indian society and equate feudalism with the Sāmanta system prevalent in early India from the eighth century A.D.

Onwards, R.S. Sharma, *Indian Feudalism*,[11] Delhi, 1965, (2nd Rev. Ed. 1980), is the only monograph, which deals with the origin and growth of feudalism in ancient Indian history, discussed the feudal polity and economy during, Pālas; Prathihāras; Rāṣhtrakaṭas and Delhi Sultan. He covers a period of about nine centuries, and mainly dealing with the political and economic aspect of feudalism, his work is the first attempt to cover the entire period. He presents a lot of information coming from his analytical publications, such as, his work shows that the critical characteristics of a feudal formation are found in the social structure of early medieval India, and dominated by a class of landlords who claim and collect rent from the peasants on the ground that they are owners of the land. He further argues that a class of subject peasantry and every peasant family constitutes the smallest unit of production and other meeting its needs of subsistence pays the remainder to the landlords.[12] The peasant actually possess the land but were compelled to pay rent in kind, cash or labour to the landlords, but the rent and labour services were collected by the donors not with the object of promoting production or the economic growth of the country but only for their own consumption, they pay not because of expectations of turn but because of custom, coercion, legal sanction and ideological influences.[13] The socio-economic formation that we have in early medieval times is the concomitant of a predominantly agricultural economy in which local needs were satisfied locally and in which the scope for the functioning of the market system was extremely limited.[14] Romila Thaper's work, *History of India,*[15] Vol. I, 1966 (Rep. Delhi, 1990), is an unquestionably one of the most considerable contribution. She has contributed a full chapter on feudal system in India, her information is extensive, and what is more important on feudal system and agrarian relation, her judgement is normally extremely sound, her views are effectively and clearly expressed. But she lives a couple of escape avenues open for herself. On the one hand she has guarded herself by asserting that, "Indian Feudalism did not emphasise the economic contract to the same degree as certain types of European feudalism", on the other hand she has kept the door open by acceptance of the orthodox liberal Marxians position, by asserting that the village were self-sufficient and did not produce any surplus. She mentions that large merchant guilds distributed goods through elaborate networks and brought these goods to the place of manufacture. She suggests that the use of the term feudalism has been contested, since the type of feudalism in India was not identical with the feudal system in other parts of the world, but the basic requisites of feudal system were present in India. She seems to be a quite uncertain about the mode of production which prevailed in Indian history. D.C. Sircar, *Land System and Feudalism in Ancient India,*[16] Calcutta, 1966 and *Landlordism and Tenancy in Ancient and Medieval India, as Revealed by Epigraphical Records,*[17] Lucknow, 1969, certainly is a proof of the author's learning and extensive reading. His works are well arranged, well-balanced and comprehensive review of land system, which cover almost ancient and Medieval India, 'he is not inclined to accept feudalism in Ancient Indian History'. He is of the view that "landlordism" has been confused with feudalism. He further argues that in the feudal system of Europe. The king was regarded as the holder of all the land of the kingdom, much of the land being let out by him to the Barnos or tenants who in return for the land, agreed to perform certain services for the king and were under the obligation of making some payments and supplied on occasions. But majority of the character discovered all over the country record grants of land to Gods and *Brāhmaṇas* without stipulating any obligation of the donees to the donors. The donees were exempted from all kind of obligations including the supply of unpaid labour. Sircar's exercise is based on the wrong assumption that the pattern of land granted till recent time, continued to be the same. He mentions that "early Indian rulers sometimes granted Jāgir for the maintenance of their officers and dependents". But he qualifies these points by adding that those were not under the feudal type of obligation but he does not care to mention their nature. B.N.S. Yadava, *Society and Culture in Northern India in the Twelfth Century A.D.*,[18] Allahabad, 1973, his work does not cover the span of our study. His work is a valuable contribution to this subject, his total rejection of the loss of king or state control over donated land may be especially true in early India when land grant were less and religious in nature, but one cannot entirely rule out the loss of the state control over donated land from eighth century A.D. onwards. The author is inclined to accept the loss of revenue to the state during his period of study. Yadava has repeatedly referred to the Western Europe for making a comparison and added great details to Sharma's work studying northern India in the early medieval period.

D.D. Kosambi, R.S. Sharma, together with Daniel Thorner, brought the peasants into the study of Indian history for the first time. Irfan Habib, *The Peasant in India History*[19] (In I.H.C., 43rd, Session, K.U., 1982—Presidential Address), also throws much light on Indian peasants such as, the origin in different phases and areas; the formation of the caste peasantry; the village community and feudalism. He has presented moreover general history of Indian peasants. B. Chattopadhyay, *Essay in Ancient Indian Economic History*,[20] Delhi, 1987, author has prepared an anthology on a particular theme, (the papers presented in I.H.C., proceeding), contributors have throw much light on the changing status of early Indian economic history, and peep into any noticeable change in perceptions regarding early Indian Economy in these forms. This collection of the articles have conveyed hardly any historiographical sense, the new source material has been used resulting in the broadening of the scope of early Indian-economic history and more significantly economic history has gone beyond narrow frontiers by relating itself to areas which are general historical relevance, certain changes, had however to be carried out. S.M. Devi, *Economic Condition of Ancient India*[21] (from A.D. 750 to A.D. 1200), Delhi, 1987, she tried to systematised the economic condition of ancient India dealing with the different aspects of economy, such as, agriculture, irrigation, domestication of animals, trade and commerce, guilds, money and banking including exchanges. Her work is valuable contribution to the history of economic theories of ancient India, but the scope of the work has, however, been restricted to Northern India (750-1200 A.D.) and archaeological sources are rarely utilised.

She has discussed various aspects of economic life of the people, such as, agricultural caste, division of soil for the purpose of raising crops of different varieties, methods employed in cultivation, agricultural tools, manures, irrigation facilities, agricultural seasons for sowing and harvesting, different kinds of crops produced, their value in respect of industry. Antiquity of agriculture, various localities of agricultural goods and danger to the agricultural products have also been discussed.[22] She further made an attempt to show the different kinds of ownership that existed in Northern India,[23] discussed in detail regarding the various industries, moneylending and banking, their nature, rates and types of interest, position of moneylender and plight of the debtors and reasons taking loans. She gives the detailed description of trade and commerce, in Northern India, land and water routes, important centres of trade, danger faced by the merchant, export and import and barter system.[24] The plight of poor subjected peasant, forced labour and the feudal culture has been discussed.[25] D.N. Jha (ed.), *Feudal Social Formation in Early India,* Delhi, 1987,[26] this work is a simply the collection of articles seeks to lay stress on various aspects of feudal social formation which have received scholarly attention. These collected articles give us the idea of Indian feudalism which is the centre of controversy in Indian historiography. These articles, by and large, give us the idea of Marxist perception of early Indian history. Jha introduced some changes to the original without interfering with the style of the individual contributor. D.N. Jha argues that the growth of feudal property in India came to be linked with the condemning of the communal right in land, as is evident from the land-grants which refer to the transfer of communal resources (*i.e.* pastures, forest, water resources, fitness etc.) to the donors.[27] The economic essence of Indian feudalism, like that of European, it has been argued, that the rise of landed intermediaries leading to the inserfment of the peasantry through restriction on peasant mobility and freedom, increasing obligation to performed forced labour, mounting tax burdens and evils of sub-infeudation.[28] It has been argued that "If the similarity in the forms and exploitation of the peasantry in Western Europe and India were present, the manorial structure is accepted as a valid basis for comparison between development in two regions, it may be stated on the basis of epigraphic and literary evidence that the peasants and the artisans were at that time attached to the soil more or less in the same way as serfs were in medieval Europe.[29]

Land-grant was an important adjunct of feudal agrarian structure in early Indian history. Om Parkash, *Early Indian Land Grants and State Economy*,[30] Allahabad, 1988, his work indicates that land-grants were not uniformly a drain on state resources; instead, they enriched the state in various ways. On the one hand, the size of the secular award found cutting across all requirements of hierarchy and peerage, and on the other hand, the awards were seem to be wholly without obligation of any kind for prospective service to be contractually discharged by the beneficiary in lieu of the grant. He further argues that the secular land-grant was determined by the material gain they brought to the state, and it is not unlikely that many of his work embodies the result of an investigation into the relationship of early Indian land-grants and state economy. His inquiry originated from the perception of the questionable nature of the most of popular explanation offered for the phenomenon of the innumerable land-grants of early India. He has noted that there is hardly any valid ground to infer the existence of a landed aristocracy of chiefs and official from these grants. It is also not possible to the prevalence of a salary prove fief system on their basis. It has been argued that the land-grants also appear to have a linkage with the state policy of imperial expansion. Om Prakash argues that land-grants not only contributed the king's share to the royal treasury but some of them also brought their prices to the king[31] but he ignores large numbers of land-grants which had been donated to donors in early India which were absolutely tax-free. He further argues that early Indian land-grants were not a drain on state economy.[32] The possibility of generating a landed aristocracy of nobles and officials is, therefore, ruled out. There is again a total absence of any condition of prospective service imposed on the recipients of secular grants. The contractual bond of protection and service between the lord and the vassal which, in one form or the other, almost necessarily characterizes feudal formation, is absolutely missing.[33] He rejects the concept of features of feudal system and his self-framed concept of the total missing of feudalism throughout the length and breadth of ancient India.

Barry Jones (tr.), *Feudal Society and Its Culture*, Moscow,[34] 1988. This work on feudal system is about the Middle Ages. The period saw the rise and decline of feudalism. The author is of the view that the history of the middle ages is the history of acute conflict between the peasants and the feudal lords. Peasant uprising took place on a scale unknown before or after in both the West and the East.[35] The author further argues that in various parts of the world, feudalism adopted various forms, and different countries and different people entered phases of the feudal formation at different times. But the economic basis of feudalism was the land which belonged to the feudal nobility. The peasants depended on the latter to work the land which they paid for in either work, produce or money. The degree of dependence of the peasantry on their feudal lords varied according to the area and the period from such extreme forms as total serfdom to merely an agreed relationship of dependence.[36] V.K. Thakur, *Historiography of Indian Feudalism: Towards A Model of Early Medieval Indian Economy*,[37] A.D. 600-1000, Patna, 1989. His work throws much light on the problems of the methodology of the study of feudalism in Indian history. Dipping deep into the well of his knowledge, V.K. Thakur has brought to our notice not only the problem of the study of Indian feudalism, but also discussed critically the recent writing on Indian feudalism. To a certain extent he sums up and makes readily available the extensive research on Indian feudalism which has gone for many years in India. Each writer is a leading specialist in his own sphere with his own evaluations of specific historical problems whom's work on feudalism he discussed. He argues that the meaning, scope and applicability of the term "feudalism" in the Indian context has been confused because of its non-discriminate use in mutually contradictory situations and widely separated chronological sequences. Such usages are completely devoid of any conceptual rigour, and view feudalism and its linguistic variants as so many people words lacking any precise body of contents. This has not only given contradictory meaning to the word; but has also led to a reckless use of terms, like "feudatory", "feudal", "feudal lord", "feudatory state," "feudatory families" etc. As a consequence the word "feudalism" by now, has acquired divergent meanings as between Marxist and non-Marxist historians.[38] The study of feudalism in the Indian context is, however, seriously hampered by the limitations of the available source material. The literacy works, however suffer from serious limitations and their nature is such that they do not provide us with clear and categorical references to the contemporary socio-economic pattern.[39] He further argues that the proper use of literacy sources becomes all the more important because of the nature of archaeological repository and tools of analysis in India. Historical archaeology is, in fact lagging far behind in respect of the material relevant to the study of the various socio-economic problems.[40]

The secular land-grant originated from this policy of imperial expansion. The loss of the religious alienation was amply compensated by acquisitions resulting from secular awards. H.K. Trevaskis, *The Land of the Five Rivers: An Economic History of the Panjab from the Earliest Time to 1890*[41] (2nd Rev. ed.) Gurgaon, 1989, the author has discussed the main features of economic life in early Panjab, evolution of economic life from very beginning. Only general survey of economic life has been given with a view to showing the progress at each step.

Johns Deyell, *Living without Silver*, Delhi 1990.[42] His work is a response to challenge of defining and exploring alternative avenues of economic research. It is concerned with money as an indicator of economic activity. Its major premise is that past economic system can usefully be defined by the pattern of production, exchange and dispersion of their money. He demonstrates that a thorough investigation of the recovered coin hoards permits a fairly coherent reconstruction of the monetary system of North India's early medieval period. He argues that during five centuries from A.D. 750 to 1250, a few superficially uniform coin types comprised monetary system startling in their complexity and diversity.[43] This was an era of base metal alloy coinage, when the precious metals were not used in form of money, but there was some regional variation in effects, the relative precious metal contents of coins was not uniform from country to country. In the Ganga basin, the high price of silver was evident as early as the eighth century, but that of gold not until the eleventh century. The silver shortage was not indicated in the northwest until the eleventh century.[44] The gold and the silver resources of North India were insufficient to support such a scale of coinage issues; only a copper was available in significant quantities. On the basis of his own analysis, he has stated that there was no shortage of currency in early medieval northern India history, but on the other hand he admits the constant *debasement* of metal content and further argued that the circulation of *daramah* was limited to the zone of Pratihara.[45] A.D. Gupta, *A History of Indian Economic Thought*, London, 1993,[46] is a latest contribution to the Indian economic life in early India, and growth of Economic institutions. Only general survey of economic life has been given with a view to showing the progress at each step in Indian economic history. He discusses in his analytical work the Indian economic thought in general, such as, Buddhist economic thought, and some details Buddhist attitudes to economic activity. He further argues the principal economic ideas contained in Kauṭilya's Arthaśāstra, laid by the Kauṭilya in respect of taxation and price policy. He devoted full chapter on economic thought in pre-muslim period, from the early part of the 13th century upto the 18th century A.D. Nothing new is noticeable in his work regarding ancient Indian feudal economy. From above brief analyses we notice that the scholars of ancient Indian economic history have opened up new lines of inquiry and imply the concept of Indian agrarian feudal structure far from being an historiographical cliché, needs further refinement and sophistication.

V.K. Thakur and A. Aounshman (eds.), *Peasantry in Indian History-I*, Patna, 1996.[47] The present collection on peasant studies, addressed to the issue of theory and structure, has decisive analytical bearing on the process of peasant formation in India. Analysing the problems of the peasants in early Indian society, V.K. Thakur's paper underlines the limitation of the conventional sources, *i.e.* the distinctly antithetical stances adopted by the two major literacy traditions — the Dhamasūtra-Smṛti centred ecclesiastical tradition and the Arthāsāstra-kāmasutra generated scholastic heritage — on the peasant related issues.[48] He suggests better appreciation as a crucial role determinant. His attempt to extend this perspective to early India leads him to the rejection of European model with a plea for a better appreciation of the element of land control in order to trim off some of the vague associates of the peasantry.[49] Thus, he highlights the highly differentiated character of early Indian peasant order. B.P. Sahu (ed.), *Land System and Rural Society in Early India*[50] Delhi, 1997. It highlights the growth and changing contours of historiography with regards to the agrarian history of early India. As such it incorporates some significant early writings as well as contributions which represent research still very much in progress. The pattern of regional socio-economic transformation in the context of wider historical developments come through in many of these essays.

The analysed historiographical trends and focuses on problems and issues, and flowing from it the areas and nature of controversies as well as on related themes. The articles included here to deal with aspects of rural settlement, the concept of village community, the problems of the ownership of land, agrarian charge, the structure of rural society and rural unrest. B.P. Sahu has been careful to draw his material from a wide range of publications, representing varieties of source material and approach. The broad area of agrarian history includes various sub-themes, and although historical writings so far available are very much unevenly distributed between the themes. L. Gopal argues that the small unit of agricultural land, was owned by individual proprieties, he has profitably utilized two inscriptions of Kangra (804 A.D.), which record the donations by private individual to a Śiva-Temple.[51] This evidence provides an example of the ownership of land by merchant, and it shows that land was owned even by classes other than those to whom grants on assignment of land were generally made by the state.[52] We come to know that there was a complete absence of the coins of some of the dynasties, such as the Pālas and Senas, Gahadavalas and Chauhan etc., do not seem to have issued a regular and complete currency in all the three chief metals and in all the denominations.[53] He further argues that the regular officials were often remunerated in the form of village grant in lieu of cash salary for state services.[54] Landed aristocrats held many of the superior past and become members of the governing body. The feudatories also directed the rural and urban economy. With the exception of Gujarat they gained control over production and distribution. As some merchants became more interested in transforming themselves as feudatories, landed aristocrats gained a measure of control of the investment capital.[55] It has been argued that social consciousness can hardly be regarded as completely divorced from social being and as such this story may reflect the actual conditions prevailing in many estates held by the donees, the *Śūdras* and *Vaiśyas* who were transferred and attached to the donees were not slaves nor all of them were village attendants.[56] The relation of dependence involving lifelong services and payment of the dues to the donees appears to have been thought of as continuing from generation to generation.[57] Thus the restrictions on mobility of *Śūdras* and *Vaiśyas,* who were peasants during our period of study, which could only strengthen the hands of the landed intermediaries and ruling chiefs in keeping peasants and other working folk under subjection.

The agrarian and economic life of Indian society saw the long and gradual process of feudalization. We notice two ways of development — on one hand there were changes in the position of agricultural commune on the other hand, the nature of the feudal estates and the right of the feudal ward over the population change. Feudal agrarian relation differed from area to area because agricultural and landless labourers, manual servants, artisans etc., were dependent on agriculture and were remunerated mostly in the common lands of the village through their status was not better than that of serfs. One question is still lingering in the minds of scholars whether artisans and peasants were attached to the soil or not? What extent they were attached to the soil? Some inscriptions indicate that the regular supply of the necessary articles from the artisans, such as, oil men making gifts of a fixed measure of oil per oilman to a temple. It shows that artisans were forcibly attached to the temples or to cater its economic needs.

The social agrarian aspect of feudal system in early India was intimately connected with the transformation of the *Śūdras*. It seems that the older settled regions *Śūdras* were provided with land, and in remote parts the tribal peasantry were annexed to the Brāhmaṇical system through land-grants. It cannot be assumed that the burden of heavily increased taxes was to put on the villagers. Many charters clearly indicate transfer of artisans and traders to the beneficiaries. These charter clearly show that the peasants, villagers and other inhabitants of the donated villages, carry out the orders of the beneficiaries. Thus, if the piece of land or village is transferred the peasants are automatically transferred. From the eight century A.D. onwards sub-infeudation has become to common phenomena in Indian history, which gave the rise to graded types landlords, different from the actual tiller of land, this also deteriorated the economic condition of the peasants. Some charters record that the donees were authorised to enjoy the land, to get it enjoyed, get it cultivated. Thus with the increase in the number of intermediaries, and peasants seem to be forced to pay additional taxes. We can deduce that the artisans and peasant seems to be attached to the soil, from the eight century A.D. onwards in India, but not in the same sense as was in Europe during middle age.

Our early Indian villages had a distinctive design which reflected closely the basic values of Indian civilization. This design had crystallized more or less during the classical phase of Indian history. Many changes were introduced into Indian society and economy. There were limits beyond which might not interchange their economic roles in the village. Member of specialist group might become agriculturists, but not *vice-versa*. It was not for just anyone in the village to become a priest, a barber, a washerman, or a carpenter or a potter. To some extent this was true, the differentiated role within agriculture. Brāhmaṇa no matter how poor, could not themselves till the land, low caste, no matter how enterprising could not become substantial landlord or priest, and it would be quite misleading to view all their members as peasants?

The donation of land to *Brāhmaṇa* and other donees, they resulted in colonization of fertile and arable tracts of land. The *Brāhmaṇas* as the highest representatives of an agrarian society were best suited for the purpose. The operation followed, as a matter of necessity, from the need for greater food production to supplement on increasing population. The land donation not only increased donees' economic status but also gave them administrative authority over such donated lands. The revenue of the concerned land was utilised by the donee, even ruler transferred to the donee all sort of rights, indicate that irrigation had become local responsibility. It seems that the body of donees had become landed intermediaries between the ruler and the actual tiller of land and inhabitants in their turn might have become the dependent on them. The ruler was not more to enjoy its right over the donated land. The donees seem to be real owners and owned their allegiance to the donees. It shows the loss of revenue and the loss of ruler control over donated village of land in early India.

REFERENCES

1. U.N. Ghoshal, *The Agrarian System in Ancient India*, Culcutta, 1929-30, he suggests that the land grants refer to the payments in kind and in cash (called *dhānyahiraryadeya*), land-grant mentions the usual list of privileges assigned to the donees, further, distinguishes the item of *dhārya* from that of *bhaga bhogakara*, both of which terms usually connote payment in kind (p. 56). He further suggests that the terms refers to *Udranga* and *uparikara* which prove the existence of state owned lands cultivated by tenants in the villages (p. 66). He argues that Chendella land-grants are concerned with endowments in favour of *Brāhmaṇas* and Temples. Their status is sufficiently indicated by a clause in one of the documents which expressly states that the donee is not to be obstructed with regard to the gift, sale or mortgage of the land. Another record which describes a family of *kaṣasthas* high offices under the down mentions that three of them received villages from

different kings. These belonged to the class of assignments granted to officials for service (p. 77).

Ghoshal argues that the land-grants of Gurjara dynasty refer to the term *udrañga* and *uparikara,* pointing to the existence of state ownership of land in the villages. An inscription of 8th century A.D. refers to *udrañga* and *uparikara*, which prove the existence of state owned lands cultivated by tenants in the villages. An inscription of the Chauhan of the year 756 A.D. mentions a king's gift of one-fourth of a village to a *Brāhmaṇa* and one-fourth to another. This evidently involved the assignment of revenue that were assessed separately upon the lands concerned.... It has been argued that the donation of three villages by three brothers of the Tomara clan who were in the service of the Emperor Mahendrapala II... and to a chief (*mahāsāmanta*) who was in possession of tract of country in central India under the same Emperor Bhoja. *Ibid.*, pp. 51-54.

2. U.N. Ghoshal, *Contribution to the History of Hindu Revenue System,* Calcutta, 1940. He has suggested that *halika-kara* might have been a tax on plough but his argument cannot be accepted because if there was the tax on cultivator or on tiller of the land, and tax on plough does not seem a separate tax on *hala* or plough.
3. B.N. Datta, *Dialectics of Land Economics in India*, Calcutta, 1952. He visited Moscow in 1921 and came into contact with the world communist movement. He discusses the socio-economic developments which took place in ancient India, he further argues in detail about the class struggle in ancient India and also is of the view the ancient Indian history also experienced feudalism. D.N. Jha rightly states that Datta was "handicapped by lack of academic training and the limited availability and knowledge of the source material not surprisingly the often interlarded his conjectures with quotations from Marx and Engels resulting in what would not appear to be a crude and schematic application of Marxism to early Indian history. Although his conclusion do not stand shunting, he is the first to have viewed early Indian society as a changing one, and to have attempted an explanation of historical developments in terms that are not peculiar to India but are of somewhat universal application. D.N. Jha (ed.), *Feudal Social Formation in Early India*, Delhi, 1987.
4. D.D. Kosambi, *An Introduction to the Study of Indian History*, Bombay, 1956, pp. 298-310. "Early Stages of caste system in Northern India", JBBRAS XXII, 1946, pp. 33-48, "The Basis of Ancient Indian History", JAOS, IXXV, 1955.
5. D.R. Chanana, *Slavery in Ancient India*, Delhi, 1960. He notices elements of slave society in early historical India, neither postulates the existence of a large scale chattel slavery in Indian antiquity. His work shows that the slaves in early India were used for agricultural as well as industrial production, which indicates that there was slave mode of production in early Indian history. "Ideological Aspects of Slavery in Ancient India", J.O.I., VIII, 1959.
6. D.D. Kosambi, *An Introduction to the Study of Indian History*, 2nd Rev. ed., 1975, pp. 295-405. His work is one of the greatest works on Indian

history. It is no exaggeration to state that this unique work on Indian history has earned universal recognition, honour and stature with a continually rising influence in the world of learning. His work does not pretend to be a history of India. It has been considered as a modern approach to the study of Indian history. He has discussed the theory regarding feudalism in two of its chapters.

7. Pushpa Niyogi, *Contribution to the Economic History of Northern India from the Tenth to the Twelfth Century A.D.*, Calcutta, 1962. She is of the views that "North Indian temples had large area of land under their direct control." She further argues that *Brāhmaṇas* and temples received donations of land from time to time. Somanath Temples was endowed with more than 10,000 villages (p. 285). The temples in some cases had, large areas of land under its possessions thus giving the organisation of status of a landlord. The king of Kashmir Kolasa confiscated the villages which formed the endowment of the Avantiskamin and other temple. It indicates that some temple in North India had vast landed property.
8. B.N. Ganguli (ed.), *Reading in Indian Economic History*, Delhi, 1964, pp. 9-18.
9. L. Gopal's work is an interesting and significant source of information covering a large range of literary and archaeological sources. At the same time it is neatly ordered and lucidly and concisely presented. He has been able to illumine a comparatively little known priory authoritatively and sought to forge a link between the ancient and medieval phases of India's history. His work throws particular light on the emergence of Feudalism in Indian History.
10. L. Gopal, *Aspects of the History of Agriculture in Ancient India,* Varanasi, 1980.

    L. Gopal, "Ownership of Agricultural Land in Ancient India", in B.R. Sahu (ed.), *Land System and Rural Society in Early India*, Delhi, 1997, pp. 95-110.
11. R.S. Sharma, *Indian Feudalism,* A.D. 300-1200 A.D.
12. *Ibid.*, p. 213.
13. *Ibid.*
14. *Ibid.*, p. 214. He rightly notices following broad developments in early medieval economy, (a) a group of individual ownership of land at the cost of royal and communal ownership, (b) subjection of peasantry through sub-infeudation, eviction, and imposition of non-customary taxes and forced labour, (c) conversion of income from trade and craft into benefices, and (d) the existence of a self-sufficient economy buttressed by lesser use of coins and comparative absence of trade. *Ibid.*, p. 109. All these may be regarded as features of feudal economy in early northern India. *Sudras in Ancient India,* Delhi, 1958, *Light of Early Indian Society and Economic,* Bombay, 1966, *Land Revenue in Indian Historical Studies,* Delhi, 1971, *Urban Decay in India,* 400-1000 A.D., Delhi, 1987. He has contributed many papers on ancient Indian economic and feudal system in various Journals.

15. Romila Thaper, *History of India,* Delhi, 1966, Vol. I.
16. D.C. Sircar (ed.), *Land System and Feudalism in Ancient India*, Calcutta, 1966. D.C. Sircar is inclined to accept feudalism in Ancient India. He is of the view that landlordism has been confused with feudalism. In the feudal system of Europe, the king was regarded as the holder of all land of the kingdom, much of the land being let out by him to the barons or tenants in chief who in return for the land, agreed to perform certain services for the king and were under the obligation of making some payments and supplies on occasions. When a tenant died, it was usual for his successor to pay a fine to the overlord before he could succeed to his estate. He argues that the Śūdra peasants cannot be equated with the unfree serf of Medieval Europe, p. 95.
17. D.C. Sircar, *Landlordism and Tenancy in Ancient and Medieval India as Revealed by Epigraphical Records*, University of Lucknow, 1969, pp. 32-35. Sircar states that the state's eagerness to get the uncultivated field cultivated and keep land under cultivation in its own interest is easily intelligible so that the tenant who cultivated the field and paid taxes regularly is scarcely expected to be dispossessed of the plot of land allotted to him for life at the formation of village. This is because it was not possible for the state to cultivate all freely acquired or reclaimed land. Not only that on the tenant's death, it would be quite normal for his son and grandson to get a lease of the same plot of land for the period of their lives successively. *Ibid.*, p. 4.
18. B.N.S. Yadava, *Society and Culture in Northern India in the Twelfth century* A.D., Allahabad, 1973, pp. 164-66. He refers the *Sakanda purāṇa* in support of his argument which leaves little doubt that hundred of people were compelled to do forced labour, and this was evidently meant for production.
19. Irfan Habib, "The peasant in Indian History" President's Address, P.I.H.C., 43rd session, Kurukshetra, 1982. He identifies a peasant with a person who undertakes agriculture on his own, working with his own implements and using the labour of his family, p. 4. T. Ray Chaudhure and Irfan Habib, (ed.), *The Cambridge Economic History of India,* Delhi, 1982, Vol. 1. This work covers the period of Muslim rule in India, and deals with the cross-sections of economic life. It has been argued that from early Eighth century to the coming of Mohd. Ghauri landholding became the chief basis of social and political status. There was an increasing fragmentation and hereditarization of local power under what was variously been termed, the *Sāmanta* system, (p. 46). It has been further argued that an increasing portion of the agricultural product was taken from the peasantry to maintain military vassals and religious grants holders, whose tenure generally survived changes of overlords. By the 10th century the consolidation of power of smaller local kingdoms is observable, with the proliferation of subordinate feudatory tenures and rights (pp. 46-47).
20. B. Chattopadhyay (ed.), *Essay in Ancient Indian Economic History*, Delhi, 1987. It has been suggested by Y.B. Singh, *Halikakara* crystallization of

a practice into a tax in above B. Chattopadhyay edited work. *Hithal hali* (begari) had been equated with *hari*. The *hal* may be equated with one of the types of *viṣṭi* tax and treated as an equivalent of *hari* system. It denotes the employment of all bullock teams under the field of a landlord for cultivating his *Sir* land without any payment. The practice gained wide currency throughout northern India and has continued even to this day. The landlords used to call upon all their lands to plough their day, that is, for one day.

21. S.M. Devi, *Economic Condition of Ancient India (from A.D. 750 to A.D. 1200)*, Delhi, 1987.
22. *Ibid.*, pp. 1-44.
23. *Ibid.*, pp. 45-73.
24. *Ibid.*, pp. 73-210.
25. *Ibid.*, p. 60.
26. D.N. Jha (ed.), *Feudal Social Formation in Early India,* Delhi, 1987.
27. *Ibid.*, p. 6.
28. *Ibid.*, p. 6. It has been argued that the kaliage is characterized among other things, by *Varṇasamkara, i.e.* Intermixture of *Varṇa* or social order, which implies that the *Vaiśyas* and *Śūdras* (peasants, artisans and labourers) either refused to pay taxes and refused to supply the necessary labour for economic production.
29. *Ibid.*, p. 12. Harbans Mukhia is critical of R.S. Sharma for visualizing "the development in almost all components of west European Feudalism. Serfdom, manor, self-sufficient economic units, the feudalization of craft and commerce, apart, of course of inform declining trade and urbanization". He argued in his paper, "was there Feudalism in Indian History." *J.P.S.,* Vol. VIII, No. 3, April 1981, p. 285. It is unfair to blame Sharma for producing empirical evidence indicating similar development in India and Europe. Mukhia himself is guilty of reading in Sharma more than his words about the existence of manor in India would mean (Sharma says *agrāhāras* granted to the *brāmaṇas* bear some resemblance to manor. D.N. Jha (ed.), *Feudal Social Formation, op. cit.*, p. 35.
30. Om Parkash, *Early Indian Land-Grants and State Economy*, Allahabad, 1988, pp. 2-3, 282-84.
31. *Ibid.*, p. 4.
32. *Ibid.*, p. 282. According to his religious grants were also converted into sources of state reverence by granting only partial exemptions implyings thereby that the unremunerated taxes were to be realised from the donee. Another methods adopted was to grant total exemption for a limited period only to the *agrāhāra* and *brahmedeya* grants in particular.
33. *Ibid.*, pp. 286-87.
34. Barry Jones (Tr.), *Feudal Society and Its Culture,* Moscow, 1988.
35. *Ibid.*, p. 9.
36. *Ibid.*, p. 13: "Feudalism arose from the ashes of the world of antiquity and the crumbling primitive communal society, elements of which served

as the building materials for new economic and cultural system. The universal charter of west European feudalism does not mean that its individual and local manifestations in the various part of the continent were the same. The new form of production, in which the small holding of the producer was subordinated to feudal ownership of the land, was common everywhere. *Ibid.*, p. 15.

37. V.K. Thakur, *Historiography of Indian Feudalism: Towards a Model of Early Medieval Indian Economy, C.A.D. 6-1000,* Patna, 1989.
38. *Ibid.*, Introduction, p. X.
39. *Ibid.*, p. XVI.
40. *Ibid.*, p. XVIII. The archaeology of the rural settlement of India is a desideratum, while material pertaining to urban archaeology is scanty. The limitation of the source also acts as a restraint to typological studies, because it fails to respond to questions pertaining to the change taking place in the society. Notwithstanding this constraint, a typological study is pertinent for a proper understanding of the complex of Indian feudalism. *Ibid.*, pp. XVIII-XIX.
41. H.K. Trevaskis, *The Land of the Five Rivers; An Economic History of the Panjab from the Earliest Time to 1890,* 2nd Rev. ed. Gurgaon, 1989.
42. Johns Deyell, *Living without Silver: The Monetary History of Early Medieval North India,* Delhi, 1990.
43. *Ibid.*, p. 6.
44. *Ibid.*, p. 7.
45. *Ibid.*, p. 65. In the Indus Valley under Arab Governors and Amirs, both copper and silver currencies were issued, but were took root. Foreign coin provided the majority of the circulating medium of small. *Ibid.*
46. V.K. Thakur and A. Aounshman (eds.), *Peasant in Indian History-I,* Patna, 1996.
47. V.K. Thakur, in *Peasant in Indian History,* pp. 123-43.
48. *Ibid.*, p. 121.
49. *Ibid.*
50. B.P. Sahu (ed.), *Land System and Rural Society in Early India,* Delhi, 1997.
51. L. Gopal in B.P. Sahu (ed.), *Land System and Rural Society, op. cit.* p. 102.
52. *Ibid.* The investigation shows that the peasant was the proprietor of land in every sense of the term. The king, as the universal sovereign of every thing in his state, had, no doubt, some claim over the land. He received revenue from the peasant as the ways for protection he afforded to the land, but this in no way amounted to a proprietary right over the land. But the question was not entirely free from discussion even in ancient times, and supporters could be found for the not much favoured view of state ownership of land. *Ibid.*, pp. 109-10.
53. K.K. Gopal in B.P. Sahu (ed.), *L.S.R.S.E.I., op. cit.,* p. 118.

54. *Ibid.*, p. 121.
55. B.P. Mazumdar in B.P. Sahu (ed.), *L.S.R.S.E.I.*, *op. cit.* p. 148.
56. B.N.S. Yadava, "Immobility and subjection of Indian Peasantry", in B.P. Sahu, *op. cit. L.S.R.S.E.I.*, *op. cit.*, p. 331.
57. *Ibid.* Yadava suggests that with the "emergence of a hierarchically organized ruling aristocracy and the weak functioning of exchange economy, especially in the agrarian set-up characterized by localism, the magnitude of forced labour naturally grew in volume during the post Gupta period. The development of Trade and Commerce and greater use of money particularly in Western India in eleventh and twelfth centuries. These economic developments may naturally have contributed to the loosening of restrictions on the mobility of peasants and artisans". *Ibid.*, pp. 335-37.

2

How Feudal was Early Indian Economy?

Economic history describes man's efforts through the centuries to satisfy his material wants. It is concerned with the age-long sequence of wants — effects — satisfaction, with wealth-getting and using of wealth. The wants start with the fundamental needs for simple food and shelter, but to those men, show with other animals, had been added a desire for more elaborate food and dwelling place, for clothing, comforts, and luxuries. Beyond these physical wants, may be the wish to accumulate still more wealth for its own sake, for the income it will bring when invested, for the sense of security it affords, or for the economic, political or social power and prestige it may confer. There may even be a continuing want of something to do, an inability to be idle and enjoy leisure, or such an intense interest in one's work that though of abandoning, it is unwelcome.

Land-grants played very important and crucial role in socio-economic formation of early northern Indian economy. The state controlled economy got transformed into a feudal economy through the issuance of land-grants which ultimately, generated a landed aristocracy as an intermediary enjoying the revenues of one or more villages. It is supposed to have brought political fragmentation of political powers reduced the peasantry to bondage and subjection, degraded the artisans and ultimately paved the way for the restrictions on the mobility of peasants and other humble folk and their subjection under the condition characterized by closed, local economy, and emergence of landed intermediaries and a hierarchy of ruling landed aristocracy are well-known ingredients of feudal economy.[1] The feudal elements might have gained importance in early Northern India, with the growing tendency to remunerate the officers in form of assignments of land. We come to know from the *si-yu-ki*,[2] and the *Harṣacarita*[3] of Bāṇa that during the 7th century A.D. the state official were mostly paid in the form of land-grants for their service to the state. It has been mentioned that Nalanda *Vīhāra* owned one hundred villages and its number went up to two hundred villages during the time of I. Tsing,[4] its number increased to five hundred villages in ninth century A.D.[5] Large number of *Brāhmaṇas* were endowed with villages on permanent basis,[6] which shows that the number of land-grants in early northern India was increasing further till eleventh century A.D.[7] It appears that religious as well as secular grants to individuals and institutions alike must have gone to long way to create a class of landed aristocracy.

Daulatputra plate of Bhojadeva (706 A.D.) records large number of land-grants to Brāhmaṇas free of all type of exemptions and hindrances.[8] Besides these many other villages had been donated to individual, priest and temples by both rulers and their feudatories.[9] The Cambay plate of Govinda IV (A.D. 930) speaks of the grants of 600 *agrāharas* and 800 villages to the religious shrines.[10] Thus, it seems that priestly institutions in early northern India have emerged as important intermediaries in land[11] between the state and the common man. The Kapadauanay grant of Kṛṣna II dated 832 A.D. records the donation of the village named Vallurika to a *Brāhmaṇa*.[12] Another donation of a village is recorded in Tokhede-Copper plate grant of Govindaraja of the time of feudatory of the Raṣtrakaṭa Govinda III, dated 812 A.D.[13] The epigraph throws no light on how did the *Mahāsāmanta* acquire the estate. This donation seems to be a secular grants from the king from all kinds of exemptions.

The Chasla Inscription of Baladitya (A.D. 725)[14] from Rajasthan speaks of the estate of Dhauagartta was enjoyed by Dhanika a chief of the Guhila tribe under the king Dhavalappadeva. K.K. Gopal argues that the division of kingdom among tribesmen was recognised even in those time as characteristic feature of the Pratihāras, and it was, therefore, natural that they formed the main strength of the Pratihāras army.[15] We come to know from an inscription from Rajor dated 958 A.D. that under the imperial Pratihāras dynasty a chief named Mathanadeva belonging to this lineage had received the village named Vamsapotaka as an allotment for his enjoyment.[16] K.K. Gopal further argues that the system of making land donation to chief of tribe continued under other clan monarchies which emerged into power during the decline of the Pratihara kingdom.[17] An Inscription has been referred dated A.D. 973, from Harṣa (Jaipur) which indicates that under the early Chauhana possession villages and hamlets which they had received as assignments from the king and which they could dispose of at will, the personal estates referred to in this inscription including those of king Simharaja, his two brothers, Vatsrāja and Vigraharāja and Govindarāja[18] (893 A.D.) records the donation of a village to a temple, without taking the approval of his overlord, Mahendrajudhadeva.[19] R.S. Sharma is of the opinion that Pāla, Pratihāra and the Rasṭrakuṭas maintained certain secular intermediaries in land-vassal officials — who were rewarded with villages for services rendered to the state.[20] Although epigraphic records show that their number was not as many as that of religious grantees. But if religious services were rewarded with land-grants, what could have been the other possible mode of rewarding secular services, especially when coins were not in common use.

The records of the Raṣṭkaṭa king Kriśna II dated A.D. 910-11 from Gujrat a group of 84 villages appears in the midst of other administrative division of longers and smaller number of villages which would suggest an attempt to incorporate the unit of clan monarchies into existing territorial system.[21] We notice a reference to a *paṭṭata* of 84 villages in the set-Mahet grant of the Gahadavala king Govindracandra,[22] and the same term *Caturasika-paṭṭāla* is mentioned in the Badera *Paṭṭals* plates of Mahanapaladeva[23] a feudatory of the Gahadavalas. *Paṭṭals* come to be used in some part of northern India as the term for a territorial division, but basically it meant the territory which the king gave to chiefs as their *Jāgirs*.[24] A Gurjara-Pratihāra records referred to the reference to the system of 84 villages. In this record the chief is said to have acquired 84 villages by the might of his own arm, probably suggesting thereby that it was not because he belonged to the same tribe that he received it but in the sense that his overlord had to accept his claim in view of his military strength.[25] A Paramāras records of the eleventh century A.D. refers to a *Sāmanta* of the Ganga family enjoying a district which was a feudal grant of 84 villages.[26] It has been argued that whatever the differences between the two sets of grantees, there is no doubt that they together constituted important intermediaries in land between the king on the one hand and the actual tiller of the soil on the other. For all practical purposes they became the occupiers and enjoyers of the villages, this gave the rise to a class of landed barons who grew at the cost, and with the sanction of royal authority over land.[27] From the three land-grants we come to know that Somavansi King Mahabhavagupta I (A.D. 935-70) had donated four villages to his Brāhmaṇa Chief Minister Sadharana, Devananda III[28], the Nanda ruler granted a village to his *kayaśtha* minister for peace and war.[29] An astrologer named Jagadhara Sarman received two villages, one from king Yasobhanjadeva of Khinjali[30] and other from the latter's younger brother.[31]

It shows that such grants were generally permanent as has been clearly received in some cases. It also indicates that these villages were donated to the donees in lieu of their salaries. These grants gave to the officers the status of the feudal chiefs. We deduce that the regular officials were often paid in the form of village grants.[32] The king Vigrahapada III[33] had donated land to a *Brāhmaṇa* officer out of his own possession with the permission of the overlord, seems to be the land donated to him as a service tenure. The similar kind of land-grant is referred in the Pala records which seems to be allotted to the *Kaivarṭṭas* as remuneration for their services.[34] However, in the epigraphic records from different parts of Northern India we often find that the state officers had title of *rauta*, *ṭhakkura* and *rāṇaka* attached to their names these title stood for feudal assignments in lieu of their salaries.[35] We notice the term *rājaṇaka* which seems to be a title of a feudal chief, was minister in the Chima (Chamba) state[36] and *Rājataranginī*[37] tells us that *rājanaka* was the little of minister in Kashmir. We can deduce that the officials were paid in terms of feudal assignments. The paucity of coins and the references to kings awarding villages to officials when pleased with them indicate a feudal economy.[38] The study of some of the lands-grants of early Northern India shows that these grants were drain on state economy. It had generated a landed aristocracy of nobles, officials and *Brāhmaṇas*.

It has been argued that the basic feature of western feudal economy was serfdom, under which peasants were attached to the soil but did not own it. In villages it gives as grants under Pālas, Pratihāra and the Rāṣṭrakuṭas the position of peasants was not materially different. R.S. Sharma argues that the religious donees, particularly the managers of big monasteries such as Nalanda, got their land cultivated by others, and their rents were collected through their agents.[39] In early Northern India donees enjoyed not only their power of sub-infeudation but also eviction.[40] In their dominions the donees had been given the right to cultivate his benefice or get it cultivated, to enjoy it or to get it enjoyed, to do it or get it done.[41] The *Skanda Pūraṇa a* work of 8th-9th century A.D., provides us very interesting information regarding the attachment of peasants to the land. According to this story king Rāma had donated a number of villages to 18,000 *Brāhmaṇa* with 36,000 *Vaiśyas* as well as *Śūdra* after performance of certain religious rites.[42]

The inhabitants of the villages, the *Vaiśyas* and *Śūdra* were directed to serve the donees,[43] who later divided the villages amongst themselves. Rāma asked the people to obey the command of the donees and to serve them devotedly.[44] The *Śūdra* and *Vaiśyas* were asked to render service and pay dues to the donees and not to leave or transfer allegiance from them.[45] We come to know from an inscription that the donees were empowered to collect from the villagers half a dozen taxes such a share of produce (*bhāga*), imposition on the threshing floor (*khala-bhiks*), a officer's dues (*Prasthaka*) *Skandhaka margganka*, resumption of property on failure of issue (*a puṭrika-dhaṇa nassti-bharṭṭa*) fee on deposits (*nidhi-nidhana*), along with all the other miscellaneous dues, proper and improper (*Uchit and anucita*).[46] This grant of land shows that the vassal treated his fellow tribesmen as tools meant for his personal enjoyment, and as tillers attached to the soil, capable of being transferred along without. The donees could be able to burden the peasant with all type of fair and unfair dues, which reduced them to the position of serfs.[47]

From the 7th century A.D. onward *Śūdras* were largely peasants in early Northern India.[48] The restrictions on the migration of peasants, which could only strengthen the hands of the landed intermediaries and ruling chiefs keeping peasants and working folk under subjection.[49] During 8th century to 10th century A.D., owing to feudal tendencies, localism backed by somewhat closed economy because so much accentuated that there developed a set of special local observances and obligations which differed from village to village.[50]

Land-grant charters bestowed the beneficiary with superior rights over and above those of taxes. The donee was entitled to collect all kind of taxes. He could collect regular and irregular taxes and fixed and unfixed payments. The donees were empowered with the right to evict the peasantry of will and to replace them with new peasants. Thus land-grants charters asking the peasant to carry out the orders of the donee as long as they are alive, it seems that peasants were attached to the land?

The paucity of coins in early northern India was the general nature of economy. But the paucity of coins during own period of study has been questioned by Johns Deyell we must keep in mind that religious shrines may not be considered the right location for coins.[51] Coins are portable item and could be offered or donated by religious devotees during their visit to religious shrines. The scarcity of coins during 8th to the 10th century A.D., appears in almost all parts of North India with a few exception in Kashmir and Punjab. As long as money was in considerable use, it was normally offered by devotees including artisans and merchant. When they became scanty, cowrie shells, which was introduced as the medium of exchange. The role of the shells as the medium of exchange was bound to be marginal. Long distance trade could not be carried in cowries.[52] The trade with middle east, all goods were valued in *dinārs* and the payment were made in the same currency.[53] Johns Deyell is of the view that the *dramma* coinage was in wide circulation during Gurjara Pratihāra rule,[54] but he also admits that its area of circulation was limited and the currency did not survive the passing of empire.[55] His statement seems to be self-contradictory. The Pratihāra inscription records several categories of coins such as *Dhamma-pada*, *Vimsopaka, rupaka, paṇa, kakim* and *Kapardaka*.[56] The *dramma* was the only coin capable of undermining the self-sufficient economy of the Pratihāra kingdom, under Pratihāra we do not know any *dramma* earlier than the 9th century A.D.[57] We come to know that the *dramma* was not used in any appreciable quantity earlier the 9th century A.D.[58] It has been argued that not a single Raṣṭrakuṭa coin has been discovered so far although they ruled for two hundred years, and their kingdom touched the sea-coast, same was the case with the Pāla to whom not single coin can be ascribed indisputably in spite of their rule for about four centuries. Nothing can be said in precision regarding the minting of copper coins in Kashmir,[59] due to the relative isolation of the country, its coinage had little impact beyond the sphere of feudatories.[60] Thus it shows that chances of the scarcity of coin in early Northern India cannot be ruled out. The main theory which strikes the student of the numismatics of early Northern India is the extreme paucity of gold coin. The Indo-Sassanian coins are not known to have been struck in gold. The Sāhi kings also struck only of silver and copper coins.[61] The silver coins of this period reveal a state of affairs which is by no means encouraging even when compared with the indicated by the Gold coins of the period.[62] Some kings and dynasties did not issue any silver coins, while other had restore to heavily debased coins.[63]

Thus, from the above survey it is clear that there was a general paucity of coins in early Northern India. The Metallic currency was almost absent in most part of northern India between 8th century to 1000 A.D.[64] The decline of trade and the grants of land to high officials in lieu of cash payment did away with the need for coins. Moreover, there is evidence for barter and the use of cowries as medium of exchange in daily transactions.

Forced labour was an important feature that contributed to the rise of feudal economy in early Indian history. The term *Viṣṭi* was used in the sense of labour, which the villagers were obliged to provide to the state and landlord or vassals.[65] During the Mauryan India forced labour was manual labourers, artisans[66] and slave, instead of paying taxes. We can understand from the use of the terms such as *Viṣṭiprādhāna, kośaviṣṭi, viṣṭiruahāra, karmantoviṣṭi, viṣṭikāra pratikarm* and *Hirangaviṣṭi* etc.[67] The labour was used for the construction and maintenance of irrigation system, for road works, fortification and other works required for the king or vassals. This labour required by the state in early Indian society cannot be referred to as forced labour in the strict sense of the term but it was by no mean a voluntary decision of an individual to work for the king or vassal.[68]

We notice *Viṣṭi* in some of the literary works of early medieval period.[69] The Rājatarangiṇi,[70] speaks of forced carriage of loads to be exacted from the villagers. In the *Kathāsaritsāgara*, villagers are mentioned as being directed by the king's officials to pluck dates from a fallen date tree. It has been argued in *Yasastilaka* by Somadeva that the viṣṭi was demanded from the villagers by the donees.[71] Some inscription of eighth and ninth centuries A.D. inform us that the village headman known as *grāmika, grāmakuta, grāmadhipati,* etc., were frequently mentioned feudal lords running their own estates with the help of forced labour.[72] Some inhabitants of the villages (*Varika*) were asked to work three days a month in the monastic estate. They had to do all kinds of agricultural works to repair and to erect monastic building.[73]

Thus, it appears that the peasant had been reduced to a state of serfdom by the extension of the practice of forced labour, and during the Pāla period the peasants were subjected to the Sarvapiḍa.[74] We further observed that vassals in eastern Kathiawad had the right to impose forced labour from the villagers, this practice was continued in subsequent times of both Pratihāras and Rāṣtrakuṭa territories.[75] The forced labour prevailed in which the donee had been given the right to cultivate the lands to get it cultivated to enjoy it and get it enjoyed. Whatever might be the factors or circumstances for the prevalence of viṣṭi (forced labour). It was very much prevalent as a considerable scale in early Northern Indian history.

One of the ingredients of the feudal economy in early India was the decline of trade, both internal and external. Silk species were important items in the Indo-Byzantine trade. The Byzantine, however, learnt the art of growing silk worms in the middle of the 6th century A.D., consequently the silk trade was badly affected.[76] The migration of silk weavers from Gujrat and their taking to other vocations acquired meaning in this context?[77] It has been argued that trade in the silk was so important in the Byzantine empire that in order to regulate silk price all-over the country Justinian (527-65) enacted that one pond of silk should not cost more than eight pieces of Gold, and that all the wealth of violator should be confiscated.[78] Justinian proposed to the Ethiopians that they should buy silk from India and sell it to the Romans, for they would thereby gain much profit for themselves and assist the Romans by serving them from having to pay their money to the Persians, who were the rivals of the Byzantine empire.[79] But it was not possible for Ethiopians to trade in Indian Silk, because the Persian merchants in the Harbours of India had Persian monopoly.[80] During the post-Gupta time the position seems to have substantially changed on account of decline in India's export and further stoppage of the supply of gold from Central Asia and the Roman Empire. It has been further argued by R.S. Sharma "Asia was completely destroyed by the Hūṇa invasion; and no gold coins are found in India for about three hundred years. When they reappear around A.D. 1000, the colonies of the pre-Turkish Muslims, who are called *Tadjiks* (Iranian), appeared in various parts of the country except in Kashmir, but no Indian colonies are reported in Persia or Central Asia from this period."[81] The Chinese account of 9th-10th centuries refers to the presence of Indian merchant in China and Chinese merchant in India in the 7th century A.D.[82] but trade seems to be confined to luxury articles and the use of countries in internal transactions referred to, by this Chinese account could not have helped foreign trade.

It has been suggested by the Moh. Habib that the Hindus were not supposed to travel overland into countries where the *munja* grass does not grow and the black gazelles do not graze practically handed over all foreign commerce to outsides, alongwith the domestic commerce incidental to it.[83] L. Gopal argues that India's share with the China was gradually dwindling probably because of the competition of Arab and Indonesian merchants. India is not mentioned among the country which according to *Suug Annals* were trading at Canton in 971 A.D.[84] The Liang-Shu does not include China in the list of countries with which central Tien-Chu had much sea trade. Obviously sea trade with China had ceased to be an important item in India's sea trade activities.[85] The frequent feudal wars of the period were also responsible for much destruction of the economic prosperity of the country.

The records of this period indicate that the invaders often attempted to cripple the trade and economy of their enemy and to destroy the lives and property of their subject.[86] It has been observed that coastal towns of India carried on some trade with countries of South-East Asia and China, but this interaction does not seems to be any intense kind. Decline of trade was just not limited to foreign trade. Long distance internal trade too suffered owing to the weakening of links between coastal town and the interior town and further between town and villages. The decay of town and shrinkage in Urban Commodity production and the decline of trade were related problem. We come to know from the *kathāsaritasāgara*,[87] a work of later period, that traders moved through forest to avoid the multiple payment of duties. Sea voyages and long distance travels were taboo. Such attitudes did not promote the cause of trade. Early Northern Indian economy experienced the rise and development of a number of rural settlement which had not been linked to exchange networks and long-distance trade. Although the exchange networks did not entirely collapse, the transfer of settlement to various kinds of donees had created a congenial atmosphere for the emergence of self-sustaining closed unit of production and consumption. Local needs came to be met locally. The growing sense of localism and self-sufficiently of the villages is to reflect its expression such as *grāmadharma*, *ghāmacāra*, and *sthānacāra* all referring to village or local practices in contemporary Puranic literature.

It is clear that early Indian villages were based on a self-sufficient economy where production approximated to local requirement, with little attempt at producing a surplus to be specifically for trade or exchange, surplus production would hardly have benefited the peasant, since it would have led to a demand from the landlord for a longer share. The existing system led to accepting the standard of minimum production, since the incentive to improve production was absent.[88] Limited production and lack of trade led to decrease in the use of coins, and trade was further hampered by the emergence of a wide range of local weight and measure, making long distance trade more difficult.[89] It has been argued that localism backed by somewhat closed economy became so much accentuated that there developed a set of special local observances and obligations which differed from village to village.[90] The Puranic literature recommend the observation of *grāmacāra*,[90] *grāmadharma*[92] and *sthānacāra*[93] with the terms *diśadhārma* and *jāṭidhārma*. The feudal aristocracy was actively connected with the accentuation of localism and regionalism.[94] R.S. Sharma rightly argued that the fundamental characteristic of feudal economy was, local needs locally satisfied, which did not leave scope for specialised production market.[95] It has been depicted that during Pāla villages were inhabited by all types of people, *i.e.* villages were populated by artisans, merchants and cultivators. The inscription of the Vaillabhattasuami 882 A.D. which records the donation revealing that peasant were not only tax-payees in the remote area, it includes artisans and traders who use to pay *kara*, *hiraṇya*.[96] Thus for the up keep of the self-sufficient economy of the village it was necessary that all sections of primary produces should live in the village.[97] This inscription further records a donation of piece of land for a flower garden, two fields, for a monthly supply of lamp-oil to be made by the guild of oil millers, and a monthly supply of flower-garlands to be made by the guild of the gardeners.[98] It seems that artisans were forcibly attached to the religious shrine of donated village. It has been depicted that grain, cloth, oil, flowers, medicine and requisite labour for the repair of building were supplied by the villages, it shows that the villages helped in sustaining the self-sufficient economy of the big monasteries by making various kinds of services available of them.[99]

Decline in trade, paucity of coins and absence of coin moulds indicate economic decline and fall in demand for finished products. Towns which were flourishing centres of trade and commerce in pre-Gupta period, experienced decay and desertion in post-Gupta times. The decline of towns and cities, is reflected in contemporary literature and inscription as well. The decline of Buddhist towns in north India attested by the account of Hiuen-Tsang who visited India during the time of *Harṣavardhana*. Hiuen-Tsang writes that the kingdom of *Rāmagrāma* has waste and desolate for many years, and that its towns were decayed with the few inhabitants.[100] He further states that the town of Ganga was in bad shape, "this town is naturally strong. It has, but few inhabitants; there are about 1000 families of *Brāhmaṇas* only.[101] He argues that the region called *Suughna* located 400 hi (miles) north-east of Thanesar, lay on the western side of river Yummina was ruined.[102] It has been depicted the Arab geographers of 9th and 10th centuries, refer to town in some parts of India but point out their fewness in the country as a whole. Merchant Sulaiman (A.D. 851) states that the greater part of India was without town, and it has been further confirmed by IBM AL FAKIN Hamdani who compiled his book *Kitabul Buldan*, state that China has large town but India does not have towns.[103]

However, the sacking of cities and towns seems to have been a common feature of the wars in early Northern India. It has been mentioned in *Rājatarangiṇi* by Kalhaṇa that Ananda, the Governor of Kramarajya, advised king Uccala to proceed to Śrinagra and plunder the neighbouring towns.[104] We come to know from the Rāja that many cities and villages were burnt by rebels,[105] it gives a vivid description of the ruin brought about by the sack of Śrinagra. The entire city was reduced to a heap of earth, full of swollen decomposing corpses. The ground was white with fragments of human skulls.[106] Thus we can surmise the nature and amount of ruins and economic decline resulting from these wars which took place during early Indian history.

It is very clear from our study that cities and towns of Gupta periods show the general trends of decline. Proceeding from east to west and north, Pataliputra, Vaishali, Katragarh, Chinand, Manjhi, Varanasi, Kusambi, Ayodhya, Hastinapura, Mathura Sonkh, Purana Kila, Noh, Ropar, Sanghol etc. show symptoms of decline.[107] We further notice that Champa Patliputra, Vaishali, Sạrnath, Bhita, etc., ceased to be towns after the sixth century.[108] Urban decline meant loss of income to the state which suffered more on account of upheavals in the countryside, since the standing army ate up a major part of revenue. Moreover, there was enormous increase in tributary vassals (*Sāmanta*) who were obliged to supply their fixed quotas of fighting contingents at the time of war. All this closely tied up with the decay of towns and trade.[109] The decline of town forced the Brāhmaṇa to migrate to the 6 villages in search of new-source of livelihood. Some of the land chartered of the early medieval India show that large number of Brāhmaṇa donees alongwith the artisans to rural areas, where they were attached to their patrons and paid in kind.[110] The decline of ancient town in early Indian history cannot be considered an indicator of decline in overall economic growth. Urban decline and stagnation resulted in agrarian expansion, which was promoted by land-grant made by chiefs and princes.[111] It has been argued that the Jajmāni system was an important element in the social organization which arose in response to urban decline, lesser use of money and agrarian expansion. The re-grouping and re-organization of social relationship affected by urban decline led not only to the rise of a class of landed intermediaries but also to the spatial and occupational immobility of the artisans by making them integral part of the *Jajmāni* system. Artisans and others were now firmly attached to the soil and their patrons. They were paid for their goods and services in kind when crops were gathered.[112] The Jajmāni system became a common practice in the Medieval Times.

REFERENCES

1. B.N.S. Yadava, "Immobility and Subjection of Indian Peasantry in Early Medieval Complex", in B.P. Sahu (ed.), *Land System and Rural Society in Early India,* New Delhi, 1997, p. 329.
2. Watters, *On Yuan Chwang I*, p. 176.
3. *Harṣacarita,* ed. J. Vidyasagra, p. 93. L. Gopal, *Economic Life of Northern India*, Rev. ed., New Delhi, 1989, p. 14. R.S. Sharma, *Indian Feudalism,* 2nd ed., Delhi, 1980, p. 91.
4. J. Takukusu (tr.), *A Record of the Buddhist Religion,* Oxford, 1896.
5. *EI*, XVII, 17, 11, 33-40.
6. R.S. Sharma, *Indian Feudalism,* In Rev. ed. Delhi, 1980, p. 91.
7. K.K. Gopal, "Assignment to Officers and Royal Kinsmen in Early Medieval India", C.A.D. 700-1200 in B.P. Sahu (ed.), *Land System and Rural Society, op. cit.,* pp. 118-19.
8. *EI*, XIX, 2, 11. 1-16 V 24, 11-6-9.

   Daulat Gupta plate of Bhojadeva I 706 A.D. The king had directed the inhabitants of donated *agrāharas* that they should obey the command of donees and pay all kinds of dues to the donees, pp. 208-13.
9. R.S. Sharma, *Indian Feudalism, op. cit.*, p. 92.

10. *EI*, VII, 6, 11-46-9 Combay *plates of Govinda IV A.D. 930,* pp. 46-47. The villages were granted together with its sources of trees, together with the cultivated soil, together with the royal share, together with all the produce such as, the produce of corns, the acquisition of Gold, the five (the proceeds of the punishments for), faults and ten offences, and so forth — and for the purpose of (supplying) the requisite materials for preparing *satta, pratisāraya* (alms-house) resources, wells, tanks, orchards and temples etc., p. 46. R.S. Sharma, *I.F., op. cit.,* p. 92.
11. *Ibid.*, p. 92.
12. *EI*, I. VIII, pp. 52-58. Om Parkash, *Early Indian Land-Grants and State Economy,* Allahabad, 1988, p. 4. He argues that the king made the grant of a village from the *karpaṭavanizza caturaśitika* (a group of 84 villages of Harsapura-750, he would not have transferred the ownership to rewardee or his successor, otherwise he would not have donated a village from it.
13. *EI*, III, pp. 53-55.
14. *Ibid.*, XII, p. 11.
15. K.K. Gopal, in B.P. Sahu (ed.), *Land System and Rural Society, op. cit.*, p. 127.
16. *EI*, 117, p. 266.
17. *Ibid.*
18. K.K. Gopal, *op. cit.*, pp. 127-28.
19. *EI,* XXXII, pp. 31-44.
20. R.S. Sharma, *I.F., op. cit.,* p. 92.
21. K.K. Gopal, *op. cit.,* p. 130.
22. *EI,* XI, pp. 20-26.
23. K.K. Gopal, *op. cit.*, pp. 130-31.
24. *Ibid.* Secular grants might be as many or more than religious but might be inscribed on palm-leaf on cloth and therefore have perished with the passage of time.
25. K.K. Gopal, *op. cit.,* pp. 130-31.
26. *EI*, XIX, No. 10, 11, 8-9. 12th century refers to Ratnapura. It would appears that Ratnapura was a feudal estate of 84 villages which originally some king had appointed to a chief of his tribe.
27. R.S. Sharma, *I.F., op. cit.*, pp. 92-93. The question arises why the religious grants are recorded on durable material. The reason is to be attributed to the fact that whereas the religious grants, meant to secure spiritual merit, were intended to last forever and were therefore recorded on durable material there was no corresponding need to preserve the land-grants made to an officer. We come to know from the *smṛtis* of *yajnavalkiya* and *Bṛhaspati* that the secular grants were written on perishable material.... It is clear that these assignments were made on perishable material such as the birch bark. In a story from the *Brhadkathākośa* similar assignments made by asking to his *Samanta* appear to have been on cloth or some such other material. K.K. Gopal in B.P. Sahu (ed.), *L.S.R.S.E.I., op. cit.,* p. 779.

28. *Ibid.*
29. *EI*, XI, pp. 32-33.
30. *EI*, IX, pp. 68-69.
31. *Ibid.*, XI, p. 73.
32. K.K. Gopal, *op. cit.*, p. 121.
33. *EI*, XXIX, No. 8.
34. *Ibid.*, No. 5.
35. K.K. Gopal, *op. cit.*, 123.
36. Vogel, *Antiquities of Chamba State*, pt. I, p. 114.
37. *Rājatrangiṇi of Kalhaṇa* (trans.) M.A. Stein West Minster, 1900, VI, 117.
38. K.K. Gopal, *op. cit.*, pp. 124-25.
39. R.S. Sharma, *I.F.*, *op. cit.*, p. 96.
40. *Ibid.*, pp. 96-97.
41. *EI*, IX, 1 plate (a) 1, 19, plate (6, 1.63, 111), p. 264.
42. *Skanda Purāṇa* (*Brahmakhanda*) 3.3.35.44.
43. *Ibid.*, 3.2.36.47.
44. *Ibid.*, 3.2.35.56.
45. *Ibid.*, 3.2.40.59-60.
46. *EI*, I, II, pp. 11-12. R.S. Sharma, *I.F.*, *op. cit.*, p. 98.
47. *Ibid.*
48. T. Watters, *On Yuan Chawang's Travels in India*, Rep. Delhi, 1961, I, p. 169.
49. B.N.S. Yadava, "Immobility and Subjection of Indian Peasantry in Early Medieval Complex" in B.P. Sahu (ed.), *LSRSEMI*, *op. cit.*, p. 331.
50. *Ibid.*, p. 334.
51. Johns Deyell, *Living Without Silver*, Delhi, 1990, p. 65.
52. R.S. Sharma, *Urban Decay in India* (*300-C 1000*), Delhi, 1987, pp. 123-24.
53. *Ibid.*
54. Johns Deyell, *op. cit.*, p. 65.
55. *Ibid.*
56. B.N. Puri, *The History of the Gurjara Paratihāras*, Bombay, 1957, pp. 134-36.
57. R.S. Sharma, *I.F.*, *op. cit.*, p. 108.
58. *Ibid.*
59. Y.B. Singh, "*Copper Coins and their Minting in Early Medieval Kashmir, A Problem*", JNSI Varanasi, XLIX, 1982, pp. 180-84.
60. Johns Deyell, *op. cit.*, 65-66.
61. L. Gopal, *The Economic Life of Northern India*, 700-1200, 2nd ed., Delhi, 1989, p. 215.

62. *Ibid.*, p. 219.
63. *Ibid.*, Gold coins are rare, silver coins are few and copper coins also are not many in number. No continuity in coin currency is noticed, nor is there any uniformity in distribution over the country. All the kingdoms into which the country had broken up, did not issue coins; nor the readers of a dynasty or kingdom seen to issued their coins. These and many such confusions mark the period and indicate at times that the coinage system had almost collapsed. P.L Gupta, *Coins,* 4th ed., Delhi, 1969, p. 82.
64. *Ibid.*
65. D.C. Sircar, *Indian Epigraphical Glossary,* Delhi, 1966, p. 379.
66. *Arthaśātra of Kauṭilya,* 11.4.
67. *AŚ* 1.4, 11.5, 11.6, 11.36, V.3, VII.1 *Manu* and *Vishṇu* also suggest forced labour. *Labour Manu Smṛti,* X. 120 *Vishṇu Smṛti*, 111.32, it has been referred in large number of inscription earlier than our period of study. *E1*, VIII, No. 6, p. 36. *The Junagarh Rock Inscription of Rudradaman* (A.D. 150) states that the Sudarasna lake was constructed with resources from the king's own treasury without burdening the people among other taxes, with forced labour V.V. Mirashi, C11, V Ootacamund, 1963, No. 6, p. 22, No. 3, p. 10, J.F. Fleet, C11, 111, London, 1888, No. 56, pp. 243-59, No. 41, pp. 196-200, *E1*, 111, p. 318, X, p. 51, XI, p. 219, XI pp. 80, 85, 174.

    T. Watters, *On Yuan Chawang's Travels in India*, 629-45, A.D. rep. Delhi, 1973, I, p. 176.
68. Marlene Njammasch, "From the Ancient labour to the feudal *corvee*, A Marxist Approach to the study of *Visṭi*" in B.P. Sahu (ed.), *L.S.R.S.E.I.*, *op. cit.*, p. 261.
69. *Agnipurāṇa,* Ch. 223. *Rājadhāṇmakanda.*
70. *Rājatarangiṇi* V, 174, VII 1088.
71. *Yaśastilaka*, 111, p. 172, V, p. 117.
72. Marlene Njammasch, *op. cit.*, p. 270.
73. *Ibid.*, p. 272.
74. *E1,* XXIX, I.b.I., 42. R.S. Sharma, *I.F.*, *op. cit.*, p. 99.
75. *E1*, XVIII, 26, 11, 66-67. XXII, 13, 1.59. R.S. Sharma argues that term *satapadyama nauistka*, produce following from forced labour on forced labour as occasion might arise, first used in the Maitaka charters was directly borrowed by the Raṣtrakuṭas. He further argues that no area and no period does forced labour seem to have been an extensive as it was in Gujrat and Maharashtra under the Pratihāras and the Raṣtrakuṭas.
76. R.S. Sharma, *I.F.*, *op. cit.*, p. 54.
77. S.K. Maity, *The Economic Life of Northern India in Gupta Period,* p. 137.
78. *Ibid.*
79. R.S. Sharma, *I.F.*, *op. cit.*, p. 54, Rich and Pankhurst, *An Introduction to the Economic History of Ethiopia,* London, 1961, p. 46.
80. *Ibid.*, pp. 46-47.

81. R.S. Sharma, *Urban Decay, op. cit.,* pp. 135-36.
82. R.S. Sharma, *I.F., op. cit.,* p. 55. S.C. Sen, Account of India and Kashmir in the Dynastic Histories of Ta'ng Period is quoted by R.S. Sharma in *I.F.*
83. H.M. Elliot and J. Dowson, *History of India as told by its own Historian,* London, 1866-77, Vol. I (Introduction), p. 46.
84. L. Gopal, *The Economic Life, op. cit.,* p. 133.
85. *Ibid.*
86. *Ibid.,* p. 254.
87. *Kathāsaritasāgara,* pp. 191, 218, 227.
88. Romila Thapar, *History of India,* I, *op. cit.*, p. 244.
89. *Ibid.*
90. B.N.S. Yadava, "Immobility and Subjection ɔf Indian Peasantry" in B.P. Sahu *LSRSEI, op. cit.*, p. 334.
91. Brahannāradya 22.11. Saka Purāṇ.
92. *Devibhāgavata Pūrāṇa,* 325.
93. *Skanḍa Purāṇa,* 3.2.40.65.
94. B.N.S. Yadava, "Immobility and Subjection of Indian Peasantry", *op. cit.,* p. 335.
95. R.S. Sharma, *I.F., op. cit.,* p. 103.
96. *EI*, III, No. 36, 11, pp. 154, 160.
97. R.S. Sharma, *op. cit.,* p. 104.
98. *EI*, III, No. 36, pp. 154, 160.
99. *Ibid.,* Monasteries and temples formed wider economic unit. It has been mentioned in Nalanda grant of Dwapala that five villages were donated for providing articles for worshipping, clothing, bedding, food and medicine of the monks, *EI,* XXIII, 47.11, 39-40.
100. T. Watters, *op. cit.,* 11, p. 26.
101. *Ibid.,* II, p. 113.
102. *Ibid.,* I, pp. 137, 318.
103. Quoted in R.S. Sharma, *Urban Decay in India, op. cit.*, p. 119.
104. *Rājatarangiṇi*, VII, 132-25.
105. *Ibid.,* 1325, VIII, 734, 1127, 1169-85.
106. *Ibid.,* VIII, 1184, 1212.
107. R.S. Sharma, *Urban Decay, op. cit.,* p. 180.
108. *Ibid.*, p. 181.
109. *Ibid.*, p. 183.
110. *Ibid.*
111. *Ibid.*, p. 184.
112. *Ibid.*

3

Nature of Peasantry in Early Medieval Northern India: An Undecided Question

The changing ideological scenario, new political compulsions and advances in social sciences did result in a growth of interest in village societies by the 19th century, but the constructed analytical models related primarily to farming as an occupation rather than to peasants as a social category. The peasant, however, forced his way into the academic would coincidentally with the increasing realization in socio-political circles about his potentiality to either sustain or destabilise an established social order. Perceptions of this linkage varied and so did vary the academic conceptualisations. The shifting stances in the scholarly discourses on peasants, at times even directly opposing and contradicting each other, more often than not, present a uni-dimensional image of a multidimensional reality.[1]

Studies of the peasantry in different places and in different era have been made by historians, sociologists, economists, anthropologists, and other scholars, all of whom use a wide variety of definitions and concepts. Some writers have employed the term "peasant" to characterize entire societies; others have dealt with the peasantry as a part of society within a longer whole. The word "peasant" has been coined in French society, came to be widely used in English from the 15th century for one who worked on the land and resided in countryside.[2] However, peasant as an object of study remained ignored for a long time in sociology. Rural sociology, which emerged as a full-fledged discipline first in the United States as early as the beginning of this century, had focus on the occupation farming.[3] Teodor Shanin,[4] argues that the study of peasantry was started in central and eastern parts of Europe during the first quarter of the 20th century. Peasants formed the largest segment of the society in Europe. They lived a life characterised by utter poverty and backwardness and the issue of their modernisation became a serious challenge to the intelligentsia there. The latter naturally turned their attention towards understanding the nature and life of peasantry.[5] Daniel Thorner argues that the prevailing practice includes analyses of peasant behaviour at the level of whole social system, nations, sectors, villages, households, and individual cultivators.[6] He further argues that peasants are usually seen as forming part of a structured society, within which they fall between the aristocracy or great landholders, on the one hand, and the landless, on the other. However, this definition has been stretched at both ends. Some writers including among peasants group of cultivators with no class of landlords above them; other refers to the landless peasantry with regards to the land which they till, the legal status of peasants may be that of proprietors, tenant, or crop sharers. They may or may not be free to leave the land.[7] In a broader sense, the peasantry has constituted the most numerous social group in all organized states, from ancient to modern times, that have rested on traditional forms of agriculture. The term 'peasant' is one of those major, indispensable, useful, and therefore imprecise and hard to define words, like capitalism and socialism. No practical definition of the term peasantry is possible there are as many definitions of this term as there are scholars who have worked or still working on this subject. Its content is primarily economic, but as with the other two terms, certain sociological associations or implications are very strong and some ideological attachment appear to be indissoluble. Peasantry in fact is a prejudicial word — people tend to have fixed ideas which they hold uncritically about what constitutes a peasant, and a great deal of confusion is created by seeking to establish an unnatural degree of precision for this convenient and general, but inexact, term. The problem of definition, which cannot be wholly avoided, can however be reduced to manageable proportions and almost circumvented by first considering the different but not unrelated, contents, within which the word is most frequently used.

At a high level of abstraction the peasantry can be dealt within the context of a peasant system of production, or peasant economy. There have been eras when the peasant enterprise was the prevalent institution, and the peasant system was the predominant mode of production. In this context the peasantry have become strongly associated with a certain stage of economic development and here the greatest degree of, confusion about the meaning of the term arise, often because of an unrecognized change in the level of abstraction. At a high level of abstraction it is very convenient to equate the period when the peasant economy was the dominant mode of production with a certain stage of economic development.[8] However, it has been argued that folk-sophisticate contrast, is central to a cultural analysis of peasantry,[9] some of the scholars are of the opinion that more important than this contrast between the peasant and the landlord, therefore, they give priority to an economic and ecological analysis.[10] The peasant effectively controlled the land on which he worked — thus, absentee landlords cannot be designated as peasant. Production is primarily for household consumption, but a peasant sells his crops, the surplus, for obtaining the things he does not produce *i.e.*, salt, kerosene, oil, utensils, clothes, medicines, etc., and for maintaining his status.[11] V.K. Srivastava argues that a village cannot be equated with peasantry because there are autonomous and independent tribal villages. All the villagers are not peasants. He further argues that there are group of people which do not practice agriculture. The "sociology of agriculture" cannot be interchangeably called the "sociology of peasantry" because of a clear distinction between the farmer and the peasant. Rural sociology does encompass peasant sociology, but peasantry can be an independent specialisation. In some cases, one may clearly distinguish peasants from non-peasants.[12] However, there are examples where the status of a person as "peasant" is conditioned by the ecological cycle. For some months he is a peasant, for other months he is not, if one strictly follows the definition of peasantry in term of agricultural producers to conceptual problems further multiply when it is in thought or taken for granted that the peasants are real growers.[13] Raymond Firth, argues that a peasant lives primarily by cultivating the soil, he is not a landless labour, but has individual right or collective claims over the land, he further argues that when we come to the orient, the criterion of agriculture is posed with problems. Depending upon the ecological cycle, the peasants become small scale producers such as cultivators fishermen and rural craftman.[14] Firth broad based conception of the peasantry cannot be accepted to many who limit the peasants to non-independent agricultural producers. Subhadra Channa is of the view that the term peasant always poses difficulties in anthropological literature, there is a confusion between what generally understood as peasant and its theoretical definition. Difficulties surface when the concept of peasantry which evolved in the European situation is applied to the Indian context. The Indian historical situation with its caste based social organisation poses a set of different condition for defining peasants. It has led some to altogether reject the usefulness of the concept for the Indian situation.[15] She further argues that Indian peasantry is not undifferentiated. Peasant do not belong to particular castes. Households fall into different caste strata. Since no village has all the caste, relations between different villages challenge the much acclaimed notion of "self-sufficiency".[16] V.K. Thakur argues that the term used for peasants in early Indian literature, though, more often than not, lacking connotative sophistication and definitional rigour, tend to convey a somewhat similar perception of the existing reality.[17] The usages of the terms, *gahapatī* and *kuṭumbin / kaṭumbika,* depicted in early texts, if explained contextually as well as semantically, put it in a hierarchical and somewhat functional separation from such terms as *kinaṣa, kriṣivala, kṣeṭsativa kriṣika, kārsaka* etc.[18] The term like *pamara, holavahaka, daśa-kammakāra* etc. add another dimension of this problem.[19] These terms also recognise the element of land-control as vital to any attempt aimed at laying bare the dynamics of the structured relations in the countryside. The *pamaras*, the *holavahakas*, and the *dasa-kammakāras* were landless groups but their labour was crucial importance for sustaining the mechanism of agrarian production will make their blanket exclusion from the peasant category unwarranted, and, in turn, shall disorient our perception of production relations in the villages.[20] Thakur further argues that these terms undergo changes in their respective connotations with the passage of time, the element of land-control which remain a key hierarchy — determinant, requires a qualified inclusion of landless group in the peasant category. Ignoring this reality will amount to negating the emergence of certain key components of the structured peasant society.[21]

During the 20th century new sources came into being, such as, Smṛti literature, epigraphical sources and Indian textual material like the Arthaśāstra of Kauṭilya, this gradually began to alter the earlier perceptions of village communities in the historical literature. However, the terms of analysis and the subject matter of study continued to revolve around land ownership patterns and revenue systems.

The historical dimension ignored by other social scientists has been included in the definition of Marxist but with some limitations. The Marxist definition of peasants as semi-feudal or feudal tenant removes this category altogether from areas in the 20th century.[22] The Marxist definition does not include within itself, for example, landless agricultural labourers whose presence in the countryside they prefer to treat as a product of capitalist penetration rather than an inherent feature of peasantry itself.[23] But the landless wage labourers have been an integral part of Indian village for a long historical period. One of the Marxist scholars, Irfan Habib defines a peasant with a person who undertakes agriculture on his own, working with his own implements and using the labour of his family.[24] Irfan's definition of the peasantry is acceptable to Marxists scholars in India, he classify the peasant such as, the rich peasant (with extensive use of hired labour), the middle peasant (mainly using family labour) and the poor peasant (with land insufficient to absorb the whole of the family labourer).[25] He identifies another type of peasant, based on property relations, and recognizes the peasant proprietor, the peasant with some claim to permanent or long-term occupancy, and the seasonal share-cropper, as separate categories. But in his views the landless labourers are not peasant, they form with peasants the working agricultural population, and their history too remain for him a part of peasant history.[26] He ignores the factor of land control and thus implies that a peasant may be an owner, a tenant or, in a broader sense, even a labourer without any right of ownership or occupancy. Such a definition makes the peasant a vague category limiting him by some only to the owner-cultivator and stretching him by other to include even the landless labourers. This vagueness of scope has led to such a broadening of the concept that in certain quarters peasantry has come to be virtually equated with the rural society itself.[27] It has been suggested that the peasant category would include in addition to the tillers of the land all those who live by the various forms of labour which are associated with a community of tillers.[28] It can be deduced from above analysis of various definitions that the inhabitants of the village may also be called peasant by using a very wide attribute of the term. These include rich land-owners, landless labourers, artisans, craftsmen and so on.

Thus, the term "peasant" has undergone many changes in meaning in the past and is still subject to various interpretations. Common to all the shifting meaning, however, is a view of the peasant as a tiller of the soil to whom the land which and his family works offers both home and a living. Peasant economy in this broad sense is already found in the earliest stage of history of all non-nomadic societies. In this period the peasant household is dependent almost solely upon the product of its own labour, a self-sufficiency which in some remote regions it has presumed to the peasant time. Its core is the family, whose size and structure have varied considerably in course of the succeeding centuries. Some characteristic differences between peasant family types, such as those driving ultimately from material order, have finally become extinct.[29] A.M. Lorenzo argues that there is a great variation of the type of peasant establishment owing to differences in economic motives and varied formation of the social order in which the peasant of different countries live.[30] We find that there are rather important differences between an Egyptian *Fellah* and an American Farmer, a German *Bardebauer* and an Italian *Mezzadro*, a Russian *Moujik*, a French *Fermier*, and Indian *kṛishak*, *kṣetrapati* and *kanṣakas* etc.[31] "The peasant population most commonly consists of the field workers. The term *kṛishak* represent the labour of the following classes, cultivating owners; landless agricultural labourers; tenant cultivators, field workers. Therefore, the present definition is limited to actual tiller of the land in all or anyone of the above capacities.[32]

The ancient Indian literary sources do not present king and peasant in a bilateral relation, which is defined more precisely is, firstly, to raise produce, and secondly, to pay a share of his produce to the king. By performing these obligation or duties, he can expect the king's protection, and he can enjoy the balance of his produce.[33]

The Sanskrit terms *kṣetrapati*, *kṣetraswami, kṣetrika* and *karaṣakas* etc. are derived from Sanskrit language and which have been depicted in ancient Indian literary as well as epigraphically sources time and again, meaning as peasant, farmer, share-cropper, the owner of the land and the actual tiller of the land.[34] In western culture a peasant is associated with a class of agricultural labourer of medieval Europe. Although the relationship of the European peasant to the land varied with development and decay of feudal society in different regions, the general characteristics of peasantry are everywhere similar.[35] The ancient Indian term *Kuṭumba-Kṣetra* occurring in the land-grants has been taken to mean the field which the cultivation owned absolutely.[36] But the evidence of medhatithi suggests that *Kuṭumbi* was a share-cropper also. The term *Kṣetrapati, Kṣetraswami, Kṣetrika* occurring in relation to the Kanṣaka[37] in ancient Indian literature used in different context. However, we observe that there was a large number of peasant proprietors who till their own land and the task to tilling the land was alone by almost all the Indian society. The *Kṣatriyas* and *Brāhmaṇa* along with *Vaiśyas* and *Śūdras* are found engaged in agriculture activities, the bulk to the *Śūdras* worked as agricultural operations.[38] Thus it can be deduced from the above analysis of various definitions that the village may all be called peasant by using a very wide attribute of the term. These includes rich-land owners, share-croppers, tenants, landless labourers, artisans, craftsmen and other who were engaged in any kind of agricultural activities in ancient India.

The peasantry might have originated in pre-historic period, cannot be said anything in precision regarding its origin in India. The primitive people might have spent the larger part of its labour-time on the cultivation of plants and harvesting of seeds. In this process not only the food gathers turn into producer. It has been argued that Megalithic communities like those of *Chopni-*

Mando among the Vindhyan foot-hills who consumed wild rice, belong to the pre-history of agriculture. Domesticated plants came with the neolithic revolution, and two zones where crops were raised have been identified within India. The first is the Belan Valley itself where grains of cultivated rice and bones of domesticated "cattle" and sheep-goat have been found for the period 6500 to 4500 B.C. — and the lowest levels give bones of wild animals only.[39] In India agricultural revolution and the first urban revolution in fact coincide in Indus civilization, the plough cultivation has been noticed and the plough indicates large extent of Indians agriculture.[40]

The Rigveda suggests the ox drawn plough, and barley is the chief food grains; but rice seems to have begun to be cultivated in the upper Indus basin. Pastoralism seems to have become more important, for the Aryans converted wealth chiefly in the form of cows, house and camels, along with slaves.[41] Whatever may be the mechanism of land control, the surplus still came from peasants. The word for cultivators, *kṛiṣti* and *charrani,* were often employed for Aryan folk as a whole, the peasants were masters of their own fields. But such 'free' peasants belonged to the superior tribes a larger segment of population would seems to have comprised the subjugated *dasya* communities compelled to part with grain and cattle.[42] It has been argued that the next stage in the history of the Indian peasantry is dominated by the clearing of extensive tracts in the Gangetic basin. Agricultural condition in the Gangetic basin were vastly different from those of the Indus culture. The bounty of the moonsoon liberated the peasant from narrow strips to which alone the flood gave fresh doses of moisture and silt.[43] By the middle of the first millennium B.C. the long period of agricultural penetration eastward had created a complex social formation marked by peasant communities created within tribes, Interspersed with settlement of servile or semi-servile labourers working under owning masters, while hunting groups enjoyed a fresh-though passing economic importance.[44] We notice that around 500 B.C. there was an immense acceleration in the process of change for almost 500 years, which universalized peasant production and also simultaneously created a caste-divided peasantry. With the introduction of iron tools for agricultural purposes, it would be proved the turning point in the history of peasant.[45] The *Jātakas* mention estates of 100 *kariṣas* worked with the help of slaves and hired labourers, the cart-owners with a wealth of 800 millions, and the veritable "cattle magnets", along with big *Brāhmaṇa* land-owners.[46] The term *gahapatis* is referred in Pali texts time and again, who ranged from the wealthy *Mahāśala Brāhmaṇa*, addressed as *gahapatis* by the Buddha and recipients of extensive, tax free, arable land as donation, to those who paid taxes — the wealthy land-owners who cultivated their farms with the help of slaves and hired labourers.[47] It is depicted in the *Arthaśatra* that the new area was brought under cultivation with the help of *Śūdra* peasants and low class elements.[48] This newly cultivated land constituted the king domain (*śitā*), which was divided into categories.[49] The first was cultivated by the labourers of different categories under the direction of the royal officers.[50] The second type was based, by one interpretation to labourers who had nothing to contribute but the labour of their bodies and surrendered ¾ of the produced to the king, and by another to those who lived by valour and paid only ¼ of the produce.[51] The second kind of land was based to share-croppers, having only temporary control over land, who cultivated it for half the produce.[52] The *AŚ* depicts that *Śūdra* could own land.[53] *Manu smṛti*[54] refers the iron plough share, which made easier to any peasant to afford iron axe to clear fresh land for cultivation and with the help of iron plough shares and more and more land could be brought under cultivation. The *kāmasūtra* refer to the headman exacting forced labour from peasant-women and compelling them to fill his granaries and work in his fields.[55] We observe that the peasants were the main tax-payers: during the Mauryan, Gupta and post Gupta times. What resulted from the breakdowns of the tribal system was not a single peasant caste, but a large number of peasant *Jātis*. By the 7th century A.D. Yuan Chwang suggests the peasants simply as *Śūdras*.[56] I-tsing shows that usually the Buddhist monasteries too leased out their lands to sharecroppers, giving them sometimes oxen, but never anything else. He further depicts that 1/3 of the total produce was brought in by the tenants. The priests were free to divide the work among servants, and keep in mind that the farming is properly done, some time force is used by the priest to compel hired servants to work properly.[57]

The fundamental feature of western feudal economy was serfdom, under which the peasants were attached to the land but were not the owner of the land. In early northern India (800-1000) the status of peasant seems to be similar. It was due to the practice of sub-infeudation. We notice from a copper-plate inscription of early northern India that an official had granted land out of his possession without the permission of his overlord-Vigrahapala III.[58] It shows that the grantees enjoyed not only the power of sub-infeudation but also of eviction. In Rajasthan, Malwa and Gujrat, the beneficiary was given the right to cultivate his benefice of get it cultivated, to enjoy it or get it enjoyed, to do it or get it done.[59] It has been argued that in early northern India the ruler and his religious grantees could expel tenants from land, and get his land cultivated by others. R.S. Sharma argues that the eviction could be practised by the king in the villages directly under his control, being men on the spot the grantees could exercise this right more effectively.[60] It seems that in early northern India, the peasant did not enjoy security of tenure. It has been stated in law-book of Vyasa (*Vyāharamayukha*) that sometimes there were as many as four stages of intermediary landed interest between the king and the cultivators.[61] Rajor Inscription of Mathanadeva of 960 A.D., reveals us that the tiller of land were absorbed in the feudal set up and were made to pay all the dues which the local peasants had to pay.[62] This inscription shows that the donation was made out of his personal estate — named (*Vamsapotakdhoga*).[63] The grantee was empowered to collect all type of taxes from the peasants, such as, a share of produce, imposition on the threshing floor, officers dues, resumption of property on failure of issue, fees on deposits, along others proper and improper dues.[64] It is very clear in this inscription that the feudal lords treated peasants, as tools meant for his personal enjoyment. It further makes the things clearer that tne donee could burden the peasant with fair and unfair taxes, which reduced them to the position of serfs.[65] We observe that the peasants who cultivated the land did not have any say in its transfer and that the peasants could not leave the soil in case of its transfer. This dual provision appears to be contradictory so far as the beneficiaries who enjoyed the discretion of removing or detaining the tenants.[66] The *Kaman stone inscription*[67] of about 905-6 refers to the donations of three plough measures of land, which was previously cultivated by the *Brāhmaṇa* (*Sahulla Jojj*) but at the same time the land was cultivated by ploughman called Eduvaka.[68]

We observe that under the grantee the peasants not only suffered from loss of traditional agrarian rights but also shown sub-infeudation and subleasing, levy of additional taxes, and forcible attachment to the land, eviction leading to in service tenancy rights and in position of forced labour.[69] It was the absence of any legal method or machinery by which the peasants could secure redress of their grievances against the donees.[70] Thus, it shows that most of the early northern Indian grants enjoin the peasant to fulfil their obligations towards the grantees by paying them all taxes and carrying out their orders. It has been argued that irrational facilities were not out of the reach of a common peasant but in some cases it was used by opulent cultivators. In his helplessness the common peasant could but pray the heavens for rains.[71] The common peasant had the basic knowledge of weather for casting on the basis of astrological calculations. This knowledge must have been a great help to peasants. He could time the sowing and ploughing.[72] As peasant was expected to know the requirement of his field as regards seeds.[73] The peasants were also required to know how seeds of particular types were to be sown, thickly or sparsely,[74] and the cultivator used to sow the seeds in the time of filling through a cone attached to the pole of the plough.[75] The *kṛṣiparaśara*[76] recommends various implements for proper cultivation to the peasant. As we observe that a large numbers of implements of the agriculturists for agricultural operations have been enlisted in early Indian sources and peasants were considered as the supreme perpetrator of agriculture.[77]

However, the *Smṛtichandrikā*[78] provides us important information regarding the methods of cultivation which the peasants should apply. The peasant had a very busy time during the harvest season. That is why a king is asked not to demand forced labour from the peasants. If he asked otherwise, that was called oppression.[79] Medhatithi states that peasants should have adequate knowledge of the method of sowing all kinds of seeds, he further suggests that the peasant should have knowledge of distinguishing between barren soils and soils capable of producing good crops. The peasant was also required to know the area and measure of corn to be sown in the field.[80] It shows that the suggestions of Medhatithi were to be followed by the peasants. The peasants knew that it is useless to sow seeds on barren land. We come to know from an inscription that the proper seasons were taken into account for cultivation by the peasants.[81] It seems that in early northern India sometimes peasants harvested two crops, like present day peasants. *Smṛti Chandrikā* discusses the function of cultivators and peasants. It has been stated that it was an essential part of his function to protect what was sown, and peasants should be alerted to protect their crops at the time of ripening against all sorts of depredations.[82] The agriculturists should have the reaped plants with their ears stacked on threshing floors with the help of their servants and attendants. After having the crops threshed, the peasants should gather the assorted staff. It has been suggested that the peasant should carefully sift the superior grains from the inferior stuff by means of winnowing fans. The peasants should carefully pressure the grains in suitable pots. Therefore, the peasants should systematically weed out the wild grass and weeds out other injurious bushes like *munja* from their fields.[83] The experienced peasants are directed to preserve the seeds of grains and plants, a cultivator is directed to take the well-riped seeds of various kinds, dug them in the sun and preserve them in various kinds of vessels. The peasants whether *Brāhmaṇa, kṣatriya, vaiśya, śūdras* or of mixed caste are directed to buy and stare the seeds of various grains.[84] *Kaśyapa* mentions that an experienced peasant should either do the tilling on the digging of pits according to the requirement of his field. He further suggests that the cultivation of paddy is best done in countries like Kosala where the fields were irrigated with river water. Therefore wise peasants, who have decided upon reaping a harvest of different kinds of rice like *Kalamā* and *Vrehi*, should first irrigate their fields well by means of channels drawn from reservoirs, rivers or lakes and dams with the help of oxen.[85] The peasants should order the uprooting of the wisps of paddy seedlings which have already been grown closely in a separate nursery, and then, tying together each wisp, he should go on auspicious hour, transplant by the help of servants in rows.[86] *Kaśyapa* has mentioned that the peasants should continue to observe the development of the sap frequently and should regularly water their field sap the proper times for the sake of increasing the sales.[87] The peasants who know his business should also collect and preserve the straw, dried blades and stalks, etc. paddy, *adhāka, maṣa,* wheat, gram which provide sustenance and nourishment to cattle in all seasons and keep them health and fit. The experienced peasants or cultivators should cultivate all cultivable commodities like paddy, *Adhāka,* pepper etc., in different kinds of soiling fields situated near the villages, towns and cities and suitable for the growth of each commodity, according to the local usage and in proper time and manner.[88] It has been argued that the peasant should cultivate delicious vegetables like *Jaṭika, poṭolika, sakaṭa* and turmeric. The peasants had been directed to grow delicious fruits.[89] Thus *kṛṣiparāśara* indicates that sometime peasants were not allowed to produce whatever crops they liked.

The *Mahāpurāṇa* indicates that the *Śūdra* constituted the bulk of the peasant class.[90] This class appeared to have included the temporary as the evidence of pleasant[91] *Medhathithi*[92] suggests, the share-croppers, the produce showing peasant. There were hired labourers like the plough drives.[93] Thus the widespread practice of granting one village or a piece of land to a *Brāhmaṇa* or any other person must have led to the emergence of a class of landlords or the cultivators in normal times. Baden Howell[94] and R.K. Mukherji have referred to a phenomenon which may be regarded as applicable not only to the later history of Indian history but also to early Indian. When the connection of a chief or individual is with a limited land, it generally tends to turn into personal and propriety connection, especially when it became hereditary. The *Brāhmaṇa* grantee who belonged to a religious class and also the common individuals, who received land-grants, could in some cases become like chief. B.N.S. Yadava argues that a royal priest who enjoyed 100 villages became like a *Sāmanta* (*Sāmanta tulya*). But what is more likely in that a grantee or his descendant who enjoyed a village only and held the land more directly than the chief in his greater estates, became in a sense the landlord the original title of the cultivators or soil-occupants must have been reduced to the status of share-cropper and temporary tenant.[95] And finally the growth of the class of landlord must have contributed to the decline of the economic status of the peasants in the countryside.

It shows that the holder of large estates claimed the superior right to the overlordship, over taxation was a terrible plight of the peasant. It is argued that exorbitant taxes were imposed in the areas of a feudal chief with the result that the peasants had to sell their ploughs, plough shares yokes and all other requisites of cultivation even sometime, they went to the extent of selling their children.[96] Thus it seems that the economic condition of the peasantry declined to a considerable extent. The poverty of the peasants had become a favourite themes among the poets and the writers of early India.[97] We come to know from the *Rājtaranginī* that the armies often plundered the fields of the villagers[98] and were oppressed by the royal officers.[99] However, in medieval Europe, the most fundamental phenomenon was the great estate or the manor,[100] but in the manorial economy, the practice of employment using agricultural labourers played a negligible role. The lord got cultivated his estate not by hiring agricultural labourers by allotting tenants on the condition of periodical services on his farm.[101] But early Indian Literary sources depict that the main part was played by labourers, servants who sold their labour on the basis of wage contracts.[102] It shows that the peasants in early northern India had to pay a number of taxes and were required to do forced labour, not servile tenure which was the case with the serfs, but in recognition of the authority of the chief and kings. The *Śūdras,* peasants and the field labourers occupied the lowest status under the *Caṭur varṇya* scheme. *Medhatithi* defines the legal status of the *Śūdra* that he possessed absolute right to personal freedom and property and that he could not be given away or sold like a slave.[103]

A feature of the agrarian situation of Europe had been the small average size of peasant holdings, which had been divided and subdivided as population increased. The reduction in the number of the peasants proprietors allowed, in some measure, small and fragmented holding to be recombined. To some extent, this resulted from inheritance, to some extent also from grant or lease of land in the manorial court, at which rents and fines were reduced in order to attract tenants. There was yet another factor leading to the concentration of parcels in fewer hands.[104] Many peasants inherited small sums of money and small amount of personal goods through the premature death of parents and relatives, and used them to acquire parcels of land or to round out their holdings. The peasant, whose holding was too small to support him and his family, had previously sought or on the demesne, many peasants could employ themselves profitably on their own land for a greater proportion of their time, and thus denied to their lord those services which he had never needed more urgently.[105] And so we again find that the peasant appears to have been the beneficiary of the changes in land-ownership which resulted from the decrease in population.

However, those states which were still owed ploughing duties and other servile obligations were fortunate in that way were not forced to pay inflated wage rates for their labour. Servile labour was, however, increasingly restless, and knowledge of the good fortune of other peasants merely increased the expectations of less fortunate,[106] and led them into the peasants rising which were a feature of the later period, when peasant holdings had been small and population pressed severally against the local food resources, there had been little surplus grain for the market. The difficulty in marketing his grain surplus, and the reduced income from what he did manage to sell, began to influence of the economic condition of the peasants.[107] R.S. Sharma argues that the subjection of the Indian peasantry in early medieval times, was a striking development connected with the socio-economic dimensions of feudalism.[108] The extracting surplus from the peasants for the benefit of either the king and or his secular and religious beneficiaries. They gave rise to new property relation and new mechanism of economic subordination from which there was no escape.[109]

We get new information regarding the misery of peasantry in northern India from *Brhāmaradiya Purāṇa,* that during the time of famines and oppressive taxes people in misery migrate to more prosperous areas.[110] But we come to know from the *Rāmacarita* that the peasants revolted against the tyrannical ruler. It has been argued that the literally sacked soldiers fought with bows and arrows riding buffaloes show that they were ordinary peasants. It may be recorded as peasant uprising directed against the Pāla, who made common cause with their vassals against the *kaiverttas*.[111] But, unfortunately, we cannot make too much from this isolated reference.

In medieval Europe the broad shoulders of the peasants were made to support the whole superstructure of the political and feudal hierarchy, the towns, their merchants and their craftsmen, and perhaps the heaviest burden of all — the Church. He may have been called upon for labour services on the demesne, and he paid rent in cash or in kind.[112] The burden was a heavy one and, as a general rule for exceeded what might be regarded as the economic rent for his land. It did not spring from a freely negotiated contract, it arose from the harsh necessities of the peasants, from his need for protection and from his inability to resist increased demands in a time of increasing population and growing shortage of land,[113] it has been argued by R.S. Sharma's that during early medieval period there developed the *Jajmāni* system. Since the artisans did not have much scope for the sale of their products in towns so they moved to villages where they fulfilled to the needs of the peasants who paid them at harvest time in kind. The temples and monasteries formed wide economic units, some of them comprising more than a hundred villages, donated land to there religious establishment got cultivated with the help of villagers of the donated villages. The villagers used to supply rain, cloth, and still others labour for the repair of these religious shrines.[114] Pound argues that the peasantry was the largest segment of the total population in medieval Europe. This proportion fell during later centuries, with the emergence of towns and the absorption of increased numbers in trade and craft.[115] Same was the case with the population of early Indian peasantry during later centuries.

The largest segment of society in ancient India was exploited and their economic condition seems to be miserable. The popular belief about the existence of *Rāmarājya* (*i.e.* a state offering to the people all happiness and no misery) in ancient India is no doubt largely a myth. It has been depicted in many early Indian land charters that the tenants were advised to obey the orders of the donee and to pay the donees whatever dues they owed to the off has been mentioned that the tenants shall render to the donee the offering of the customary taxes such as *bhāga-bhoga* and *hiraṇya*.[116] Some of the charters indicates that all the tenants did not enjoy the some status, the donee was allowed to enjoy the right of *Udrañga* and *uparikara*,[117] *uparikāra* means a tax imposed on the peasants who have no proprietary right then on the land.[118] It indicates that *udrañga* means fixed taxes imposed on permanent tenant.[119] The *Rājataragiṇi* of Kalhaṇa states that "Every case should be taken that there should not be left with the villagers more food supply than required for one year's consumption, not more oxen than are wanted for the tillage of their fields; if they should keep more wealth, they would become, in a single year, very formidable *Dāmaras* and strong enough to neglect the commands of the king.[120]

The early medieval Indian records indicate the heavy burden of dues on the early northern Indian peasants. The burden of taxation on the peasants increased and eleven types of dues are mentioned in Gahadavala grants.[121] If all these were changed by the state or the donees then the peasants might have left with even a bare subsistence. In addition to the transfer of taxes in many cases the grantees were given the right to fixed and unfixed, proper and improper taxes, and the donees were authorise to collect taxes covered by the term (adī), all sources of income. The copperplate inscription of Harshavardhana records the grant of a village to *Brāhmaṇas,* this plate depicts that the peasants or villagers are asked to pay all taxes (usual tax-*pratyaya*) along with *tulya-meya*, *bhāga-bhoga kāra*, *hiraṇya* etc. to the donees.[122] One of the land charters records that donees are entitled to impose certain taxes on the peasants or villagers such as, *bhuta*, *hiraṇya*, *bhāga-bhoga ādāna* and a *cāṭa-bhaṭa prāveśya*, etc.[123]

The Paithan plates of the Rastrakata king Govinda III 794-814 A.D. records the following taxes which villagers and peasants were supposed to pay to the donees, such as (a) *S-odranga* together with the fixed taxes on permanent tenants (b) *Sa-parikara* (together with the occasional taxes or the taxes or temporary tenants), *Sa-das-aparadha* (together with the power to deal with cases involving the ten offences), (d) *Sa-bhutapata pratyaya* (together with the income resulting from earthquakes etc., (e) *S-optadyamana-Vistika* (together with the right to utilise unpaid labour whenever die), (f) *Sa-dhanya hirary-adeya* (together with the dues payable in kind and in cash), (g) *a-cata-bhata pravesya,* (h) without the jurisdiction of any royal officer, (i) together with *abhyantara-siddhi* (internal income and revenue and (j) in accordance with the *bhumicchidra-nyaya* (principle of the fallow land or the first cultivation of land).[124] The land grant of *Chamba* which belonged to the eleventh century A.D. enjoins the tenants of the village to deliver to the donee dues like *bhāga-bhoga,* etc. and king's Cāṭas and *Bhāṭa* and directed not to enter into the donee's house, to let his vegetables be grazed on, to cut his ripe crops or crush his sugar-cane, to take cow's milk from him, to carry off his stools, benches or couches, and to seize his wood, fuel, grass etc. It is also directed that not even the slightest oppression or vexation should be caused by anyone to the donee or to his ploughmen, cowherds, maids, servants and dependants.[125] But the exemptions depicted in the record make it clear that the tenants were often subjected to considerable harassment, and it shows that there was heavy burden of taxes and obligation on the peasantry in early northern India.

It has been argued that the peasants in early medieval northern India could not leave villages which were granted to the donees along with its inhabitants. It has been mentioned in the *Brhānnaradiya Purāṇa* that the peasants were attached to the plough for carrying on cultivation,[126] the inhabitants of a village were asked to cultivate the fields, or suffer some penalty if they keep any part uncultivated and to render dues and services according to local customs, including payment of part of the produce to local officials, village artisans etc.[127] The fields, grain, cattle and other property of a peasant who leaves the villages and more always elsewhere are to be taken by the chief or king.[128] The *yuklikalpataru* of Bhoja says that the peasants must be protected and preserved in every village because the agriculture which is the source of all wealth, depends upon their labour.[129] B.N.S. Yadava rightly argues that this kind of attitude must have reinforced restrictions on the movement of the peasant and their subjection.[130] He further argues that the ruler of the period began to grant to the temples, monasteries, individual brāhmaṇa and also their officers and vassals not only the revenues of villages carrying with them authority, only in subsidiary capacity over the inhabitants thereof. But also estates with specified authority over their residents such as peasants, artisans etc. in the village grants.[131] The intensity and scope of subjection and dependence of the peasants in the Indian context were much less than the seriated of the peasantry in western feudalism.[132] V.K. Thakur argues that a decisive factor for peasant's dependence was the restriction imposed on their mobility, the peasants could not have left their respective localities, they came to be confined to their villages not by legal but economic restrictions on their mobility.[133] He further argues that despite the available instances of subjection and enserfment of peasantry, it needs to be appreciated that the free peasant did count in the production system. We have references to *bhaṭṭagamas* (bhaktagramas) as fairly large landed estates worked by slaves and servants in ancient time,[134] but the same came to be filled by dependent peasants in early medieval India.[135] R.S. Sharma argues that the *jajmāni* system was reinforced by the charters which insisted on peasants and artisans sticking to their villages. Some grants laid down that tax-paying peasants could not be introduced into a granted village from outside, the purpose of this being that grants should not disturb the self-sufficient economy of the villages.[136]

Thus, from long survey of literary as well as epigraphic sources of early India we can deduce that there was a large number of peasants who owned land and cultivated its work of tilling-land was done by almost all sections of the Indian society: the *Brāhmaṇas, kṣatriyas* along with the *Vaiśyas* and *Śūdras*. Largest segment of *Śūdras* population was engaged in agrarian operations in early northern India, worked as agricultural labourer paid or otherwise. The large number of peasant worked on the fields of big landlords. These peasants had contributed a lot to the prosperity of the country through the ages. It appears that there was a large number of temporary peasants to whom the land was leased out by the owners (share-croppers, the produce sharing peasants).

It shows that the landless peasants were assigned a subordinate status and seems to be attached to the soil and required to work as per the wishes of the landlords ? We noticed that the peasants under the donees were reduced to a servile position while the full peasant lost in status because of the imposition of several new taxes in early medieval period. The landless peasants were faced with many miseries in order to get rid of their adopted to desertion.

Sometimes people are emotionally attached to their native places, it may not be because of feudal obligation. Thus, we cannot say anything in precision regarding the nature of peasantry in early medieval northern India, this point seem to be undecided.

REFERENCES

1. V.K. Thakur and A. Aounshuman (eds.), *Peasants in Indian History*, Patna, 1996, p. 63.
2. Raymond Williams, *Keywords,* Glasgow, 1976, p. 194.
3. Hetukar Jha, "Understanding peasant and its Low-classness," in V.K. Thakur and A. Aounshuman (eds.), *Peasants in Indian History,* p. 4.
4. Teodor Shanin (ed.), *Peasants and Peasant Societies,* Harmondsworth, 1971, p. 11.
5. *Ibid.*
6. Daniel Thorner, *Peasantry,* in David L. Sills (ed.), *International Encyclopedia of Social Sciences*, New York, Vol. II, p. 504.
7. *Ibid.*

   Daniel Thorner argues that "when we search the literature of agrarian history for discussion of peasant economies we find them scattered among such diverse categories as 'subsistence', 'feudal' or 'oriental'. By contrast, we believe there is hope of rich analytical yield if we can find a way of treating 'peasant economies', as a distinctive group." Thorner, "Peasant Economy as a category in *Economic History,* in T. Shanin (ed.), *Peasant and Peasant Societies, op. cit.*, p. 202. Peasantry as a group is subject and exists to be exploited by others.... At the same time, from the point of view of production, the peasant households constitute definite independent entities. Because of this duality in their position these peasantries inevitably straddle the line between free and unfree." *Ibid.*, p. 206.
8. S.H. Franklin, *The European Peasantry*, London, 1969, pp. 1-3. Franklin argues that "the whole of Europe has now reached the stage where the peasant economy is either no longer the predominant mode of production, and in some countries has not been for decades, or it has reached the point of losing its pre-eminence. Many of the paradoxical features of contemporary peasant life are related to the exposure or creation of contradictions within

the kingship — economic orders of the peasant enterprise arising out of its incorporation within these predominantly non-peasant system." *Ibid.*

9. V.K. Srivastava, 'On the Concept of Peasant Society', in V.K. Thakur and A. Aounshuman (ed.), *Peasant in Indian History I, op. cit.*, p. 22.
10. *Ibid.*
11. *Ibid.* It has been argued that by the Wolf that the peasant primarily aim at subsistence, and when he aims at reinvestment and maximisation of gain and profit, he ceases to be a peasant. Now he is a farmer. Then what is landlord? A landlord is a peasant when he himself tills the land and aims at subsistence, primarily involving domestic labour force. But when he abstains from tilling because of status reasons, or in specific cases because of religious injunctions, and has right over produce, the term "peasant" cannot be used for him. Peasant, thus, becomes a particular historical type of the people, with dynamism at both its ends. *Ibid.*, pp. 22-23.
12. *Ibid.*, pp. 23-24.
13. *Ibid.*, p. 24.
14. Raymond Firth, *Malayan Fishermen Economy,* London, 1946. Quoted in *Peasant in Indian History* I by V.K. Srivastava, *op. cit.*, p. 25.
15. Subhadra Channa, "Indian Peasantry Some Analytical Issues", in V.K. Thakur (ed.), *op. cit.*, p. 51.
16. *Ibid.*, p. 52.
17. V.K. Thakur, "The Peasant in Early India : Problem of Identification and Differentiation", in A. Aounshuman (eds.), *Peasant in Indian History* I, *op. cit.*, p. 131.
18. *Ibid.*
19. *Ibid.*
20. *Ibid.*, p. 132.
21. *Ibid.* Uma Chokaravarti is of the view that the meaning of the term *gahapati* was shifted from a general term implying householder to a term with a more specific meaning the most wide ranging and inclusive explanation of this term, going beyond its earlier connotation as householder, is provided by the statement that except a king, or one who is in the service of the king, and *Brāhmaṇa,* he who remains is a *gahapati*.... A notable feature of the term of *gahapati* is that it is enumerated as one of the seven treasurers of the king, as the symbol of sovereignty. The *gahapati* was clearly regarded as being intrinsic to kingship. Why the *gahapati* was regarded as a crucial element in the king's sovereignty is evident from a symbolic narrative where the king requires the *gahapati* to provide him with wealth for the kingdom. The *gahapati* is described here as "one who pays taxes and thus increases the king's wealth. Uma Chokaravarti, 'was the *Gahapati* — A Peasant Producer', in *P.I.H.*, *op. cit.*, pp. 160-62. Ranabir Chakravarti, argues that two terms to designate the early Indian peasant, *viz. Gahapati* (*grahapati*) and *kuṭumbin* or *kuṭumbikā*. The two terms, *grahā* and *kuṭ umba* more or less meaning the same thing *i.e.* a House, the grahapai and the *kuṭumbikā* can literally be translated as lord of the household and one having a household respectively. Such terms are often associated with land

and agricultural activities, indicating thereby that the two terms essentially denoted peasant in the context of his family unit. The *grahapati* and the *kuṭumbikā* seem to have been distinguished from tiller of the sort, variously called *kinasa, krṣivala* and more frequently, *karaṣaka,* Ranbir Chakavarti, *Kuṭumbikās* of *Early India in P.I.H., op. cit.*, p. 181.

22. Subhadra Channa, *op. cit.*, p. 53.
23. *Ibid.*
24. Irfan Habib, "The Peasant in Indian History (General President's Address)" Proceedings of the Indian History Congress 43rd. Session, Kurukshetra, 1982, p. 4. Irfan Habib, The Peasant in Indian History' in B.P. Sahu (ed.), *L.S.R.S.E.I., op. cit.*, pp. 205-6. V.K. Thakur, in *P.I.H.I., op. cit.*, p. 128.
25. Daniel Thorner, *International Encyclopaedia, op. cit.*, pp. 503-11. V.K. Thakur, *P.I.H., op. cit.*, p. 128.
26. Raymond Firth, *Molay Fishermen,* Their Peasant Economy, cited in V.K. Thakur & A. Aounshuman (eds.), *P.I.H., op. cit.*, p. 128.
27. C. Von, Dietze, *Peasantry in Encyclopaedia of the Social Sciences* (ed.), E.R.A. Seligman, Toronto, 1950, Rep. Vol. XI, p. 48. In many regions some independent peasant household survived through the centuries the freedom of action of the peasant was early limited by territorial associations of a cooperative character, subsequently peasant fall under the rule of a landlord or other type of overlord. It is not yet very clear whether to what extent the earlier restrictions originated in the land commune.
28. *Ibid.*
29. *Ibid.*
30. A.M. Larenzo, *Agricultural Labour Condition in Northern India,* Bombay, N.D., p. 1.
31. *Ibid.*
32. *Ibid.*, p. 2. W.H. Moreland defines "peasant" as the man who, whatever, the incident of his tenure may be cultivate a holding entirely or mainly by his family labour, for his own profit, and at his own risk, sometime does not himself take an active part in production, and on the other hand from the serf whom he feeds on the hired labour to whom he pays wages. *The Agrarian System of Northern India*, Delhi, 1968, 2nd ed., p. 3.
33. *Manu*, XXV, Visnu VII, *Gautama*, 11, *Bandhayāna*, XIX, *Brismiṭi,* XXXIII.
34. *Sanskrit-Hindi-English Dictionary* by Surya Kanta, New Delhi, 1975, pp. 168-69.
35. Sir M.M. Williams, *A. Sanskrit-English Dictionary,* Oxford, 1960, pp. 332-33. He defines *karshaka,* as soil plougher husbandman, *kshetrika*, as relating to a field having fields agrarian or owner of field, a farmer, cultivator, and *kshetrin*, as term for those who owed land, on cultivating and or an agriculturist.
36. V.V. Mirashi, C11, Vol. IV, pt. 1, p. CLXXI.
37. *Yāj. smṛti*, II, 158, the *vivādaratnā kara* refer to the *kṣetrāsvāmi* and the sub-tenants on temporary occupants.

38. *Ibid.*
39. Irfan Habib (ed.), *Essays in Indian History, Towards a Marxist Perception,* Delhi, 1995, pp. 110-11.
40. Stuart Piggott, *Pre-Historic India,* 1950, pp. 176-77.
41. Irfan Habib, *op. cit.,* pp. 114-15 and D.D. Kosambi, *An Introduction to the Study of Indian History, op. cit.,* pp. 70-71.
42. D.R. Chanana, *Slavery in Ancient India,* Delhi, 1960, p. 20.
43. Irfan Habib, *op. cit.,* pp. 115-17.
44. *Ibid.,* pp. 117-20.
45. *Ibid.,* p. 120.
46. V.K. Thakur, in *P.I.H.* I, *op. cit.,* p. 135.
47. *Ibid.*
48. *Aś,* 11.1. VII. 2.
49. *Ibid.* 11.24.
50. V.K. Thakur, *P.I.H.* I, *op.cit.* p. 136.
51. *Aś,* 11.24.
52. *Ibid.* 11.1.
53. *Ibid.* 11.2.
54. *Manu Smṛiti, The Law of Manu* for G. Buhler, Oxford, 1886, pp. 420-21.
55. *Kāmasutra,* 5:5:5.

    It has been cited by Irfan Habib, that a young son of peasant like the village headman and official he has access to village women as they render forced labour, work in his field as also in his house, on taking away cotton and other fibrous material from him, bring him yarn in return. He says that this is a rare picture of exploitation of peasant by a peasant in ancient Indian country side, "The Peasant in Indian History", in B.P. Sahu (ed.), *Land System and Rural Society in Early India, op. cit.,* p. 222.
56. T. Watters, *On Yuang Chwang's Travels in India,* I, London, 1904, pp. 168-69.
57. T-tsing, *A Record of Buddhist Religion,* (Tr.) Takakusu, pp. 61-62.
58. *IA,* XII, p. 258, 11.10-15, and R.S. Sharma, *Indian Feudalism,* Delhi, 2nd (ed.) 1980, p. 96. Sharma argues that probably as a secular beneficiary he could not do this without the sanction of the king. But the religious donees, particularly the managers of big monasteries such as Nalanda, got their land cultivated by the other, and their rent was collected through their agents (p. 96).
59. *Ibid.,* p. 97. Sharma states that the same formula was employed earlier by the Maintraka rulers of Valabhi IA IX, 1, plate, al, 19b. 1, p. 63.
60. R.S. Sharma, *I.F., op. cit.,* p. 97.
61. Vyasa, *Vyāharamayukha,* p. 86.
62. *El,* III, 36, 1.4, pp. 263-64.
63. *lbid.,* III 1.12, p. 264.

64. *Ibid.*, II, pp. 11-12.
65. R.S. Sharma, *I.F., op. cit.*, pp. 97-98.
66. *Ibid.*, p. 98.
67. *EI*, XXIV, pp. 329-33, II, pp. 19-21.
68. R.S. Sharma, *I.F., op. cit.*, p. 101.
69. *Ibid.*
70. *Ibid.*
71. Lallanji Gopal, *The Economic Life in Northern India,* Delhi, 1989, 2nd Rev. ed., pp. 292-96.
72. *Ibid.*, p. 296.
73. *Kṛtyakalpatru*, *Gōrhasthyakānda,* p. 256.
74. *Ibid.* 256.
75. L. Gopal, *The Economic Life*, *op. cit.*, p. 303.
76. G.P. Majumdar and S.C. Banerji (eds.), *Kṛṣi-parašara,* Calcutta, 1960, pp. 119-20, cited also by L. Gopal in *The Economic Life, op. cit.*, pp. 304-05.
77. S.M. Devi, *Economic Condition of Ancient India,* Delhi, 1987, p. 12. Several terms have been mentioned in the inscriptions as well as literary works, such as, *okrṣakah, kutumbi, sirana, kṣetriakāra, hālika and krṣivala in gandalekhamālā"* of Sridhara, p. 16, II, pp. 48, 55,*.Saduktikarnāmṣta* and *parsistaparvan* of Hemachandra, II, p. 357. *EI*, XX, No. 13, p. 125, No. 140, p. 136, *El*, XII, p. 51, 1.12.
78. *Smṛti Chandrikā* III, Vyavahara-kānda, p. 559.
79. S.M. Devi, *Economic Conditions, op. cit.*, pp. 14-15.
80. Medhatithi on *Manu* X, 71.
81. *EI*, XX, No. 13, 1.5, p. 123.
82. *Smṛti Chandrikā* III, Vyavahara Kānda, II, p. 558.
83. M.S. Randhawa, *A History of Agriculture in India*, Delhi, 1980, Vol. I, pp. 485-88.
84. *EI*, XX, p. 125, No. 13, *Rājatarangiṇi* IV, 226.
85. *Kesapiva-kṛiṣi-suktī* of muni Kaśyapa, cited in *Agriculture in Ancient India,* by ICHR, Delhi, 1964, pp. 66-64.
86. *Ibid.*
87. *Ibid.*
88. *Ibid.*, pp. 66-70.
89. M.S. Randhawa, *op. cit.*, pp. 488-89.
90. *Mahāpurāṇa,* XVII, 164. *Grāmā urithpari krapsatra syvruchitaksya Śūdra ksrbhūmibsta sarama silāśya.*
91. B.N.S. Yadava in D.C. Sircar (ed.), *Land System and Feudalism in Ancient India,* Calcutta, 1966, pp. 90-91.
92. *Manu Smṛti,* IV, 253, *Viṣṇu Smṛti,* LVII. 16, and *Yāj. Smṛti,* 1.166, mention that the Śūdra share-croppers were entitled to half of the crop. But

the *Br. Smṛti* and the *Vyavahārakanda* (p. 4010 of Laksmidhara in which it has been cited lay down that *Sirāvāka* should get 1/3 or 1/5 of the produce, cited by Yadava, in D.C. Sircar (ed.), *LSFAI, op. cit.*, p. 91.

93. Vivādaratrākara (p. 158) *Laksmidhara* explains the term *kinaśa* as plough driven, sometimes *kinaśa* has been depicted as *kṛṣibala*, p. 124, and it has been suggested that they got 1/10 of the produce.

94. Baden Powell, *Land System of British India*, Vol. I, pp. 134-52 and R.K. Mukerji, *Land Problem of India*, p. 29.

95. B.N.S. Yadava, in *LSFAI, op. cit.*, pp. 91-92.

96. *Ibid.*, p. 92.

97. *Avadānakalpalata* of Kṣemendra, XXIV, 94-96.

98. *Rājatarangiṇi*, VIII, 168-70.

99. *Narmamālā* of Kṣemendra.

100. Paul Vinogradoff in *Cambridge Medieval History*, Vol. II, p. 649.

101. E. Lipson, *The Economic History England*, pp. 83-84.

102. *Vyavahārakāṇḍa* of Laksmidhara cited by B.N.S. Yadava in D.C. Sircar (ed.), *LSFAI, op. cit.*, p. 94.

There are sections on the employment of labourers and servants and the wage contracts. Different kinds of agricultural labourers like the *Śiravahakas* (Crop-sharers) *kṛṣibalas* and others are mentioned.

103. G.N. Jha, Medhatithi on *Manu*, p. 231.

"Yadi śūdro vidhamāndhna khātnuiṇ jūvid brāhmaṇadhanpāksitona jātu duṣipti na hi trya dānādhankriya yujgtī krutghjā ddāṣut".

104. N.J.G. Pounds, *An Economic History of Medieval Europe*, New York, 1974, p. 444.

105. *Ibid.*

106. *Ibid.*, pp. 444-45.

107. *Ibid.*

108. R.S. Sharma, *I.F., op. cit.*, pp. 217-18.

He argues that the position of the peasant was the imposition of forced labour. In Mauryan period slaves and hired labourers were subjected to such labour. But from the 2nd century A.D. the practice seems to have been extended to the class of subjects.... In Bengal and Bihar peasants were subjected to all oppression (*Sarvapidā*) from which exemption was granted in the villages given to religious donees by the pala.

109. *Ibid.*, pp. 118-19.

110. P.M. Sastri (ed.), *The Brahāmnaradiya Purāṇa*, XXXVIII.

111. *Rāmacarita of Sandhyakaranandi* II, 39-42. *El*, XXIX, 5. Sharma discussed that we have hardly anything else to illustrate this form of reaction on the part of the peasants. The usual form of reaction therefore may have been migrations. But these could not be of much avail in the face of the self-sufficient, almost closed, economic system which the peasants were tied down in early medieval times. Economic condition and political organisation

being basically the same everywhere, migration did not liberate the peasants from the oppression of the princes and beneficiaries. *I.F.*, p. 220.

112. N.J.G. Pounds, *op. cit.*, p. 164.
113. *Ibid.*
114. R.S. Sharma, *IF*, *op. cit.*, p. 121-22.
115. N.J.G. Pounds, *op. cit.*, p. 164.
116. *C11*, Vol. III, pp. 118, 122, 127, 137,
117. *Ibid.*, pp. 105, 109, 120, 128, 132, 138, 170, 185, 189, 218, 257, 290.
118. *Ibid.*, pp. 128, 132, 138, 170, 290.
119. *Ibid.*, pp. 238, 246.
120. Rāj IV. 347-52. This statement is cited by D.C. Sircar, *Landlordism and Tenancy in Ancient and Medieval India* as Revealed by Epigraphical Records, Lucknow, 1969, pp. 62-63.
121. D.C. Sircar, *Select Inscription*, Vol. I, pp. 408-9.
122. *EI*, Vol. IV, p. 414. Consult Harṣa ins. Bansakara.
123. *Ibid.*, XXXIV, p. 176.
124. *Ibid.*, III, p. 109.
125. Vogel, *Antiquities of Chamba State Part-I*, pp. 167-69 and also cited by D.C. Sircar, in *LTAMIREK*, *op. cit.*, p. 74.
126. Hazra's (Tr) *Brahāmnaradiya Purāṇa*, 38.43.
127. B.N.S. Yadava, 'Immobility and Subjection of Indian Peasantry' in B.P. Sahu (ed.), *LSRSEL*, *op. cit.*, p. 333.
128. *Ibid.*
129. *Yukṭikalpatarn*, Calcutta, 1917, p. 6.
130. B.N.S. Yadava, *op. cit.*, p. 335.
131. *Ibid.*
132. *Ibid.*, p. 336.
133. V.K. Thakur, "The Peasant in Early India," in A. Aounshuman (ed.), *PIH.I*, *op. cit.*, p. 141.
134. *Ibid.*, p. 142.
135. *Ibid.*
136. R.S. Sharma, *IF*, *op. cit.*, pp. 121-22.

4

Land-Grants and Their Impact on Early Medieval Economy

Land-grants played very important and crucial role in the socio-economic and political formation of early northern India, it was an important adjunct of feudal economy of pre-feudal period which got transformed into a feudal economy through the issuance of land-grants and generated a landed aristocracy. It has been argued that it brought about the transformation of political power, reduced the peasantry to bondage and subjection, degraded the artisans and ultimately paved the way for the conquests and subjugation of India by many foreign elements.

However, the land can be variously classified as cultivable, cultivated, fellow, barren, low, high, hilly, marshy merely, etc. There were also land fit for becoming a house site (water), land reclaimed from river-beds, etc. But from our smṛti point of view, the land of the country could be divided into the following categories : (1) state land, (2) land in the occupation of tenants who paid the king's dues according to agreed rates, and (3) land in more or less uninhabited and uncultivated areas, over which the effectiveness of state control varied under different circumstances. Each of these categories could be subdivided into different types.[1] D.C. Sircar argues that the state land could be divided into five categories, such as : (a) land attached to the king personally; (b) fiefs allowed to members of the royal family, officers and subordinates, etc., (c) land cultivated by state farms, (d) land cultivated by ārdhikas who were temporary tenants receiving half the share of the produce for their labour, and (e) uncultivated and waste land of various types.[2] In early India, the king was generally regarded as the owner of all land, and the tenants enjoyed the right of building and occupying houses and of cultivating the fields on payment of certain dues to him. But the king's rights in respect of the ownership of land were often relegated, in various degree, to the vassal, fiefs holders and privileged tenants who may be regarded as landlords under the primary ownership of land, *viz.*, the king. However, there was a difference of opinion between two groups of early Indian writers as regards the king's ownership of land. One of these two schools, represented by *Jaimini, Śabara* and others held that the state was not the owner of all land, but was only entitled to buy taxes from the holders of the land.[3] "The whole earth cannot be donated by the king. The ownership of the various villages and fields in the entire earth or in a province belongs only to the holders of the land, while the kings are entitled to collect taxes only,[4] on the other hand, the second, even acknowledging the king's responsibility to protect his subjects, lays emphasis on the concept that the king is not only the embodiment of various divinities and a great god in human form, but that he is the owner of all the *surva-bhumer-adhipatir-hisah.*[5] Megasthenes, considers all India as the property of the king and no private person was permitted to own land.[6]

The use of the term 'benefit' in Medieval Europe was to describe the land granted in lieu of service and in particular vassal service. The land had been granted to the lord's serjeant on a condition that he should exercise faithfully supervision over the tenants or to a painter in returns for decorating the Church of monks when he served; or to a carpenter or a goldsmith in the understanding that he would henceforth place his skill at the disposal of the lord or to a parish priest as a payment for exercising the cure of soils or finally to vassal; the armed comparison of his land and warrior by profession.[7]

The granting of land in lieu of services was the central principle of feudalism in Western Europe. The king was regarded as the owner of all land, much of which he let out to his barnos on tenants in chief who, in return for the property, agreed to perform certain service and to make some payments and supplies. This was usually to provide the king with a specified number of soldiers in times of war. The barons, in their turn, let out land to others on similar conditions, and same process was continued down the scale.[8] Om Prakash rightly argues that no other single phenomenon has been ascribed so much causal value in early Indian history as that of the land-grants. Feudalisation, ruralisation, regionalisation, stagnation and backwardness of early Indian society, economy and state are traced back to a single factor, that of the land-grants.[9] However, the word can be defined as rural or agricultural area, as contrasted with urban ones, and the factor of production consisting of all natural resources. It is evident from the early Indian texts and archaeological sources that the king made donation to temple, monasteries, monks, *Brāhmaṇas* and their religious and other secular individuals as a reward and salary for their religious and other services, on a recognition of their learning. In course of time the idea behind the donation of land got changed. It became an accepted phenomenon to grant-land in lieu of cash salary. But land donation in India is still a matter of controversy for obvious reason. Many questions were raised *e.g.*, why did early Indian King's supported land-grant; even the practice had invariably hit their economic interest, caused loss of revenue and loss of state control over the land granted to the donees. Land-grants are carefully drafted legal documents of their time. Within their limited scope they are supposed to provide us a first hand knowledge of the historical past. Land-grants are taken to be highly reliable sources and their evidence is taken almost on its face-value, unless, however, there are unmistakable indications of fraud detectable in a particular case.[10]

Generally two kinds of land were donated to the officials, *Brāhmaṇa* in lieu of cash salary for their services to the state *e.g.* pasture on barren and land lying in the outlying regions of the state. The purpose of these land-grants may be many, the king might have sincerely desired to bring uncultivable land under cultivation, secondly by granting the land in the far flung areas where the royal authority was little felt by the presence of central authority. Thus the king could exert its influence in such areas where the people were oblivious of central authority prior to the grant was effected. R.S. Sharma opines that the land-grants are noticed in such places where the circulation of coins were either minimal or absent. This argument although had relevance but we cannot say emphatically that it was because of absence of coins that land was granted. It might be owing to the desire of the king to bring more and more land under cultivation through donees.

While assessing the merits and demerits of land-grants in view of state position, we can say that the state could exert its influence in such areas where it was unknown, secondly by means of land-grants a new class of landed aristocracy emerged in the society and they were successfully rallied behind the state. However, the demerits of such land-grants can be seen in the light of loss of revenue that the state suffered and also the loss of state control over its land created the problem of sub-infeudalism. It was common in early northern India that the villages and plots of lands were granted to *Brāhmaṇa*, Buddhist monks, religious establishment, such as, monasteries, temples, even secular person too. We find very few instances of land-grants in later Vedic[11] and *Dharma sutras*[12] period, land-grants were made as a *daṇa* (pious gifts) and donors wanted *puṇya* out of that *Bhudana* (Land-grant). But Manu recommends the land-grants to the *adhipati*[13] of villages. Kauṭilya suggests land-grants to *Brāhmaṇa* and some state officers.[14] It shows that the fashion of making land-grants in Indian history was as old as *Brāhmaṇa* and Buddhist literature. It has been used in different manner and capacity in different periods.

The epigraphical sources of early India indicate significant changes in the relation of the donors and the donees and consequently its impact on the state. *The Nirmanḍ copper plate inscription of mahāsāmanta and Mahārāja Samudrasena* (612-13 A.D.)[15] records the grant of the village of *Sulisagrama* by *Samudrasena* to a body of *Brāhmaṇas* who studied the *Atharva Veda* at the *agrāhara* of Nirmanḍa near the bank of the river of Satluj in Kulu district of Himachal Pradesh for the god Tripurantaka of Śiva with all type of immunities, for the establishment of *bali, cara, sattera* etc., and for the supply of the materials for daily worship of the god. The grant was made perpetually. This Inscription tells us that the grant was made to the donees, together with the level and march and forest land, together with the inhabitant, with the *udrañga* (and) including all its boundaries, grass, timber and springs,[16] etc. This shows that the grant was made along with the inhabitants and they seem to be attached to the soil, but not in the same sense as was in Western Europe. *The Sahpaur Stone Image Inscription of Adityasena* (7th Century A.D.) refers to the gift for religious purpose by satapaksa in the agrāhara of Nalanda free from all hindrances.[17] *The Banaskhera copper-plate inscription of Harṣa*,[18] records the donation of the village named Markatasagara to two *Brāhmaṇas* of *Bhāradvāja goṭra*. They were exempted from paying all dues with all immunities; the *Madhuban Copper-plate Inscription of Harṣa* (631 A.D.)[19] refers to the grant of the village called Somakundaka to Somavedi Bhatta.... Vatasvarmin of *Samrni goṭra* and *Ṛgvedi gotra*. It was away from the Vāmarathya who had been enjoying it on the strength of a forged document. The village was donated to the donees with full right of inheritance by Harṣa. The grant of Harṣa states that a village was donated in favour of two *Brāhmaṇas* as an agrāhara (rent free holding usually in the possession of *Brāhmaṇa)* in accordance with the custom governing its acceptance by *Brāhmaṇa* so that the customary privileges going with such holding remained understood. The villagers were asked to be obedient to the donees and to pay them the all dues (*Pratyāya*) including *tulya, meyabhaga, bhoga, kara, hiraṇya*[20] etc.

We come to know from the *Midnapore copper-plate Inscription of the time of Sasanka* (600-25 A.D.) which refers to the grant of 20 *droṇas* (*droṇavapas*) of ordinary land and one *droṇavapa* of homestead land in favour of the Madhyandira *Brāhmaṇa*.[21] The *Midnapore copper-plate Inscription of the time of Sasanka*,[22] refers to the donation of the locality named *mahā-kumbharapadraka* in favour of the *Brāhmaṇa* of the *kaśyapa goṭra* free from all hindrances. *The Kailan copper-plate inscription of Sridharanarata* (665-75 A.D.)[23] records the donation of 25 *pāṭakas* of land made by the king was transmitted to the *vishayapatis* of the two *vishaya* called *guptinataṇa* and *paṭalayika* and their *adhikarṇa* (office) by the kumāramātya stationed at Devaparvata and by their *adhikarṇa*. The grant was made at the request of the *Mahāsāndhivigrahika* jayānatha and the gift land was dedicated to the Bhāgavat Tathāgataratna (Buddha) or Ratnatraya for the worshipping of the Buddha, the reading and writing of Buddhist religious texts and the provision of food, clothing and other accessories for the

Ārya-sangḥa as well as to a member of *Brāhmaṇa* for the performance of their *pañch-mahāyajna.*[24] The *Ashrafpur copper-plate Inscription of Devakhadga* (670-85 A.D.),[25] records the grant of several plots of land, measuring 9 *Pāṭakas* and 10 *droṇas,* by king Devakhadya, in favour of the Buddhist monastery. One of the plots of land is stated to have been in the *Jāgir* held by queen Prabhavati and another is that of the *Sāmanta* Vantiyoka.[26] The *Deo-Baranark Stone Inscription of Jivitagupta II* (C 700-10 A.D.) records the grant of a village in favour of the god varunavasi-Bhattaraka,[27] the grant was made together with the *udrañga, upanikara*, proceeds of fines for ten offences, and other income.

The Khalimpur plate of dharmapaladeva (775-82 A.D.)[28] records the grant of four villages to a temple of the god named Nārāyaṇa, free from all hindrances. This copper-plate Inscription depicts that all the important dignitaries assembled at four villages, such as, the *Rājans, Rājānakas, Rājaputras, Rājāmatyas,*[29] *Senapati, viśagnapati, Bhogapātis, Śakaśṭādhikriṭas,*[30] *Danḍosaktis, Dānḍapātyas, Chauraddhāraṇikas, Darhsadhasādhanikas, Deltas khōlas,*[31] *Gañgamikas, Abhītuaramanus*; Inspector of elephant, horses, cows, buffalo-cows, goats and sheep, inspector of the forces *Tarikas,*[32] *Saulkikas, Garlanikas* were dependent of the king's feet. Sometimes, some of them who belonged to the irregular and regular troops ask to present from time to time to the chief writers,[33] *Jayaśthakayaśtha mahāttaras, Dāśagrāmikas*[34] and other district officers were forbidden to enter into the donated villages.[35] Thus we notice that these four villages were donated with their *Lattika* and *talapātaka*[36] with all types of exemption. The villagers and cultivators were directed to pay all kind of revenue to the donee instead of paying to the state.[37] The *Nalanda copper-plate inscription,* (812-50 A.D.), records the donation of five villages, named *Rajagriha* (*Rajpur*), *Nandivanaka, Manivataka*, *Natika* and *Hastigrama* (in district Rajgir), and one in the Gay Visaya (district Gaya).[38] It shows that villages were granted with all kinds of exemptions, such as, exempted from the entry of the *Chāṭas* (Village-officers) and *Bhāṭas* with taxes dues to the king's family or court, nothing of these to be recovered, according to the *bhūmichchhidra*, and last as long as the moon and the sun would shine on this earth.[39] The *Barah-copper-plate inscription of*

Bhojadeva (C 836 A.D.)[40] refers to the donation of *agrāhara* named *Valakagrāhara* which lay in the *Udumbara* Viśaya of Kalanjara-manḍala, in the Kānyakubja-bhukti to the *Brāhmaṇa* born of the family of *Bhaṭṭa* kacharara swamin belonged to the *Bhāradrāja-goṭra* and a student of the vājasaneya-śākhā with all its income. The inscription tells us that, owing to the incapacity of the controlling officer in the time of Rāmabhadradeva, it was disturbed for the sometime and the Bhojadeva, the grandson of Nagabhatadeva, revived it on the old terms on 18th October, C 830 A.D.[41] and this document shows that the *agrāhara* was granted with all types of exemptions and residents of the village were directed to be obedient and pay all the dues to the donees.[42]

A. Cunnigham discovered two inscriptions in 1846 in the famous temple of Śiva-Vaidhyanātha at Kirāgrāma (Baijnath) in the Kangra district of former Punjab (now in Himachal Pradesh) from the Paleographical point of view, he assigned the date of these inscriptions about 804 A.D.[43] We find some references to land-grant made by the secular persons to the temple of *Śiva-vaidyanātha* at the village of Kirāgrāma.[44] The Praśasti No. I, records the grant of land which was made by a Brāhmaṇa named Ganeśvara, son of Govinda and inhabitant of Kirāgrāma. He donated half a plough of land to the temple in Naragrama, where he possessed a field which required four droṇas of seed corn,[45] we notice in the same Praśasti that a rich merchant Jivaka son of Depika and Mathika, donated his own land in Kirāgrāma for the courtyard in front of the temple.[46] However, it has been mentioned in the Praśasti No. II that Rajanaka Lakṣman Chandra and his mother made a grant of one plough of land belonging to the village named Pralanmba, on permanent basis.[47] It is clearly stated in the Praśasti that grant of land must be protected as long as this earth exists.[48] We notice in the *Praśasti* No. II, that two merchants named Manguka and Ahuka donated one plot of land cultivated by four plough along with oilmill and one shop in Kirāgrāma to the temple for the maintenance of lamp,[49] it further suggested that land belonging to Naragrāma had been donated along with the inhabitants.[50] The *Monghyu copper-plate inscription of Devapala,* 9th Century A.D.[51] refers the grant of a village Meṣikā situated in the kṛmila-viśaya to a *Brāhmaṇa.*

The Pandukesuar copper-plate Inscription of Calitasura (824 A.D.)[52] records that Paramabhattaraka Mahārajādhiraja Parameśvara Lalitaśuradev informed all the officials assembled there, together with the officers in change of the township inhabited by the eighteen kinds of subjects, headed by the *Rājam, Rājanaka, Rājaputra, Rājāmatya, Sāmanta, Mahāsāmanta, Thakkura, Mahāmanaśara, Mahākārthākritika, Mahāpratihara, Mahādaṇdanāyaka, Mahārajāpramātara, Śarabhāñrga, Kumāramatya, Uparika...Tadāyuktaka, Viniyaktaka,* superintendents of the elephant, horse and camel troops, *Duta, Preśaṇika, Daṇḍika, Daṇḍapāśika...*cowherd, merchant, and foremen of guilds to all the inhabitants, to the entire people, to the regular and irregular soldiers etc; that some land which was lying within the jurisdiction of the administrative unit called *Thappalasare* forming a part of district was donated in favour of god with all type of exemptions. *The Partabgarh Inscription of the time of king Mahandrapala II of Mahodrya* (C 946 A.D.),[53] records the various grants made by different authority to the monastery of Hari-Risisvara, who originally belonged to Dasapura. Under its management were the shrines of Vata-yaksini Devi, Indraditya or Inderajaditya-deva and Trailokya mohanadeva, which were situated at the village of Ghonta-varsika, where there was a temple dedicated to Nityapramditya-deva.[54] This inscription depicts that a village was donated by Mahārāja Mahandrapala II in favour of Vata-yaksni Devi.[55] the second part of inscription records a grant of village, in favour of Indradityadeva by Mahadeva, the provincial governor of Ujjain, at the request of Chahamana Indra-raja, a feudatory chief.[56] Third part of inscription of a field in favour of Indrarajaditya-deva by Bhahtri-patta, son of Khommana donated in 942 A.D.[57] and the fourth part of document refers to the land-grants to different deities by different persons, the gift of a field named Chhittullaka, in which 10 *Manis* of seeds could be sown, and which was irrigated by one leather bucket, in favour of Indraditya-deva, the donation of a field was made Indra-raja to the god Trailokyamohanadeva. The donation of a field, in which 10 *manis* of seed could be sown, and of Mochha field, requiring 10 *manis* of seed was made to unknown diety.[58] *The Paschimbhog plate of Srichandra* (C 925-75 A.D.)[59] records the various land-grants. D.C. Sircar, divides this document into three block, first block depicts the donation of 120 *pāṭakas* to the *Gaud Brāhmaṇ* for *mātha* or temple, it shows that the *mātha* was a big religious establishment out of the said land, 10 *pāṭakas* were allotted to teacher for exposition of the *chandra*[60] (*Chandrayakarana*), 10 *pāṭakas* for the pali (maintenance) and ghuṭika (chalk etc.) of 10 students, 5 *pāṭakas* for daily offering of food to 5 (guest) *apurva-atithe. Brāhmaṇa, pāṭaka* to Brāhmaṇ who built the temple; 1 (one) *pāṭaka* to the accountant or astrologer, 21 *pāṭakas* to the scribe (kayaśtha), 1 *pāṭaka* to 4 *florist* (malakarat), 22 *oilmen,* 2 *potters* (Kumbhakāra), 5 players on the drum called *katala*, 2 conch-shell blowers (Sankha-vadaka), 2 players on the big-drum called *dhakka,* 8 player on the *dragada* (Kettle-drum), 22 servants (Karmakana) and Cobbers.[61] Two *pāṭakas* to the dancer (nāts), 2 *Pāṭakas* to each of the 2 carpenters (sutradhāra) to masons (*Sthapati*), 2 blacksmiths, 3/4 *pāṭaka* the land to 8 maid servants, (devadāsi), and 47 *pāṭakas* for repairs to be carried in the temple establishment.[62]

The second block of inscription refers to the 280 *pāṭakas* of land in favour of the gods.[63] The details of the distribution of 280 *pāṭakas* is depicted in lines 42-47 of the document which speak of the following persons — attached to the two groups of four *māthas,* 10 *pāṭhakas* of land was donated to each of the 8 teachers of the four *kedas* (*i.e.* 80 *pāṭakas* in all), 5 *pāṭakas* for each group of 5 students in each of the eight *māthas* (*i.e.* 40 *pāṭakas*), ½ *pāṭakas* to each of the following in each of the eight *māthas* — the *flourist,* the barber, the oilmen, and washermen, servants and cobblers (*i.e.* 16 + 32 = 48 *pātakas*), ¾ *pāṭakas* to each of 2 maid-servants in each of the 8 *Māthas* (*i.e.* 12 *pāṭakas* in all), 10 *pāṭakas* of land for repairs to each one of the 8 *Māthas* (*i.e.* 80 *pāṭakas* in all),[64] two *pāṭakas* to *Mahāttara Brāhmaṇa* (chief priest) in each of 2 groups of māthas, 2½ *pāṭakas* to the scribe of each 2 groups of māthas, and 1 *pāṭaka* to the astrologer, an accountant of each of the 2 groups of māthas, 3 *pāṭakas* to the physicians (Vaidya) attached to each of 2 groups of māthas, thus this account for 280 *pāṭakas*.[65] D.C. Sircar is of the view that the third block of land was left over after the distribution of first and second blocks (measuring 120+280 =

400 pāṭakas) were donated in favour of 6000 *Brāhmaṇas* headed by the following thirty-seven names.... Vasusadatta, Harṣra, Sekhara, Bhimapala, Jyeshtha Gupta, Sasidatta, Jayadatta etc., etc., the six thousand *Brāhmaṇas* received six thousand equal shares. An interesting feature of the name of these *Brāhmaṇas* shows that the family names of many of them were stereotyped name ending and were such as are prevalent now among the non *Brāhmaṇa* communities, *e.g.* Datta, Naga, Nanden, Pala, Ghosa. It has been suggested that most of these *Brāhmaṇas* having the present non-*Brāhmaṇas* were later merged in the non-*Brāhmaṇa* communities — like the *Vaidya* and *Kayaśtha.*[66]

We notice that these donations have been made in accordance with the principle of *bhūmichchidra-nyāya* with libations of water as a permanent gift lasting as long as the moon, sun and earth would exist, with certain privileges, together with all the income enjoyed by the state in the shape of taxes in kind and cash. The cultivators and the peasants of the countryside are directed to be submissive to the donee and to pay them the proper dues. The *bhoga-patis,* landlords (governors) of the future are also directed to approve that grant and protect if considering the greatness of the merit occurring to gifts.[67] Since, the Inscriptions being the valuable records of bestowing the gift of lands, villages. From above survey of epigraphical sources of early Northern India, we are able to deduce that the grant of lands and villages with inhabitants, house-sites, cultivated, uncultivated fields, genders etc. etc. to the *Brāhmaṇas,* monks, religious as well as educational institutions, such as, *vihāras,* temples, *māthas* as also servants, and officers of the state on kings for various state services, had been donated as tax-free, donation by the kings, and private individual, subordinate rulers and state officials in lieu of cash salary. K.K. Gopal, rightly argues that "in the 7th century A.D. the state officers were mostly paid in form of land-grants, and this would appear to have been the common practice in our period as well."[68] D.C. Sircar inclined to accept the *Feudalism* in early Indian history and not inclined to accept to donation of land to any state officer.[69] On the other hand he admits that "there are a few charters recording grants of land to people of the warrior and other classes for service provided to the king."[70]

He also admits that early Indian rulers often granted Jāgir for the maintenance of their officers and dependent.[71] He too, qualifies his argument by adding that they were not under feudal obligation; he however, fails to explain the nature of obligation. His argument seems to be theoretical in nature. He states that Indian society was class and clan-ridden and left no scope for the development of feudal tendencies,[72] a suggestion which is more conjectural than factual. Om Parkash is of the view that besides their absolutely tax-free nature, the land-grant, have also been taken for granted for their entirely charitable character, bringing nothing in return to the state. He further argues that the study of the land-grants are incorrect and there are a number of instances of fixing a special tax in the land-grants themselves. The special tax has been variously termed as *tṛṇo-daka, nikara, āruvaṇa agrāhāra-pradeyāmśa, Piṇḍa-daṇa* etc.[73] Om Parkash argues that the several grants do not only the right to all the taxes and other sources of income, announcing further, the ban on ingress and egress of the regular and irregular troops in the donated villages or land, nowhere mentioned that the donee will be paying nothing to the state or Government.[74] His rejection of the concept of feudal land-grant is blunt but primarily based on whatever argument he could put forward in favour of his work. But he should keep in mind that it has not been recorded in any land charters that the donee will pay something to the state. We recorded large number of land-grants which depict various exemptions, and different sources of state income were transferred to the donees, like, grass-land and pasture land of the village, (*Sna-sīmā-tṛṇayutigocara-paryanta*), the surface of the ground (tāla), the space above the ground (*uddesa*) the dug land and water of the village (Jala-sthala) and the pits and barren spots (*gant-osara*), salt pits (levana), market places and landing station (haṭṭa-ghaṭṭa). Records of some of rulers of the Himalayan areas mention, besides boundaries and pasture lands, trees, orchards, springs and waterfall etc.[75] were the sources of revenue to the state which had been transferred to the donee and finally state suffered huge amount of revenue. Om Parkash states that early Indian land-grants were not a drain on the state economy, he further argues that religious grants were also converted into sources of state revenue by granting only partial exemptions implying thereby that the unremunerated taxes were to be realised from the donee.[76] He refers only partially privileged grant but ignores fully exempted estates or land-grants.[77] R.S. Sharma argues that "peasants could not leave cultivation and escape to other village, some villages were transferred to the donees along with artisans, herdsmen and cultivators, tied down to the fool. Perhaps the practice was rendered necessary by the scarcity of working population for running the rural economy".[78] Since, the fundamental function of the peasant is to cultivate the soil, there is no other way out except cultivating the land, and about the movement of the peasants from donated village to another village seem to be that generally, people are emotionally and sentimentally attached to the soil, they would like to stick to their respective place under any circumstances? Om Parkash, however, argues that the state somehow left helpers under the pressure of immemorial tradition of the non-taxability of the *Brāhmaṇa* to abolish their time *honoured* prerogatives,[79] but we did not get any idea regarding the helplessness of state which compel state to grant land to *brāhmaṇa* and religious establishment with all type of exemption. He himself admits that there was feudal formation and hierarchy of officials paid in terms of land assignments.[80]

It has been argued that "an" inscription of the 10th century from Gorakhpur clearly says that the village which the minister granted to the goddess Durga, had been received by him through the favour of king Jayaditya, most probably a feudatory of the Gurjara-Pratiharas. It would appear that some times the king pleased with an officer for some valuable service performed by him gave a village over and above the usual remuneration he was receiving.[81] An inscription which belonged to 973 A.D. from Harṣa (Jaipur) indicates that under the Chanharas of Sakambhare the kinsmen of the king had in their private possession villages and hamlets which they had received as assignment from the king and which they could dispose of at will.[82]

It has been directed in the Nirmaṇḍ copper-plate inscription that the villagers who so long paid taxes to the donor would henceforth have to pay them to the donee.[83] It shows that the grant transferred of the donor's revenue income etc., from the villagers to the donees.[84] D.C. Sircar confuses that the gift of a village without such income would be useless to the donees. He qualifies this point by stating that 'granting a village' and 'granting a village together with the villagers' thus mean the same thing.[85] Thus granting a village by donor or granting a village together with inhabitants does not make any differences to D.C. Sircar. The Paithan copper-plate of king Govind III[86] (794-814 A.D.) and the Sungal plate of king Vidagdha first quarter of the eleventh century A.D.[87] record the various exemptions to the donee.

We come to know from the charter that it is also ordered that not even the slightest oppression or vexation should be caused by anybody to the donee or to his ploughmen, cowherds, maids-servants and dependants. L. Gopal rightly observed that over-lords did not make any serious efforts to stop exaction of feudal chiefs. As the Central authority in the period had declined considerably and had to depend on the levies sent by the feudal chiefs, it could not afford to interfere with their high-handed exploitation.[88] He further argues that the overlords were aware of the chiefs and gave them some degree of approval by recognising their existence. In the land-grants of the period we some time finds the terms *ṇiyatāniyata,*[89] *Vcitānucita* and *bhauṣyat,* suffixed to the list of taxes which a donor transferred to the donee. These terms amount to a recognition of the possibility of new taxes being imposed in the future and of their being unjust in some cases. Thus widespread land-donation generated a class of landed aristocracy and feudal lords and ultimately state suffered not only the loss of revenue but also the state control over donated land.

REFERENCES

1. D.C. Sircar, *Landlordism and Tenancy in Ancient and Medieval India as Revealed by Epigraphical Records,* Lucknow, 1969, p. 3. Those who are well versed in the *śāstras* admit that the owner of the land and water and that the people can exercise their right of ownership over all other things excepting these two...unprepared land shall not be taken away from those who do not cultivate them and given to other; or they may be cultivated by the village labourers and traders; or the owners who do not properly cultivate them should pay for the loss of the state. *Ibid.,* pp. 2-4.
2. *Ibid.,* p. 3.
3. *Ibid.,* p. 1.
4. *Ibid.*

5. *Ibid.*, p. 2. Sircar argues that copper plate charters often speak of the grant of land as a rent-free holding in accordance with the *bhūmicchidra-nyāya* or the principle of *bhūmicchidra*...when the governor or a small vassal chief wanted to create a rent free holding in favour of a *Brāhmaṇ*. On a deity, he applied to the king and apparently paid the price of the land in question at least on a theoretical basis. In such a transaction, it was believed, according to an old Indian convention, that five-sixths of religious merit for the pious act would go to the purchaser of the land and one-sixth of it the king whose government alone could create rent free holding. *Ibid.*, pp. 4-7.
6. *Ibid.*, p. 2.
7. M. Bloch, *Feudal Society* (tr) C.A. Mangon, London, 1961, pp. 165-67.
8. D.C. Sircar, *op. cit.*, 32-33.
9. Om Parkash, *Early Indian Land Grants and State Economy,* Allahabad, 1988, p. 1.
10. *Ibid.*, p. 2.
11. *Āit. Brāhmaṇa,* VIII, 21 *Śāt. Brāhmaṇa,* XIII. 7. 1.15, VIII, 1.18. 1,73.4. *Chandupan,* IV. 2, 4-5.
12. *Āpastamba,* 11. 10.26, *Gautama,* V. 19, XIX.16, *Vas,* XXVIII, 16, XXIX, 10.
13. *Manu Smṛti,* VII. 115-17.
14. *Aś* 11.1, II.35.
15. K.K. Thaplyal, *Inscription of the Mankharies Later Guptas, Puśpabhutis and Yaśovarman of Kanauj,* Delhi, 1988, pp. 182-83.

    J.F. Fleet (ed.) C., Vo. III, Varanasi, 1969, No. 80, plate, X, p. 286. G.C. Chauhan, "Traces of Feudalism as seen in the Nirmanḍ Copper-plate inscription of C. 612-13 A.D." in *Annals* of (BORI), Vol. LXXVII, Pune, 1997, pp. 241-46.
16. J.F. Fleet, *op. cit.*, p. 289, Lines 8 to 10. G.C. Chauhan, *Loc. cit.*, p. 244.
17. K.K. Thaplyal, *op. cit.* No. XIII, pp. 158-59.
18. *Ibid.*, No. 17, pp. 176-82.
19. *Ibid.*, No. 18, pp. 182-85.
20. D.C. Sircar (ed.), *Select Inscription,* Delhi, Vol. II, 1983, No. 3, pp. 24-25, Line No. 9.
21. *Ibid., Yathānyāyṃ śubhkīrtire ® ym vu (BO) dha catvārīdhs (riś) dhdo dronās (droṇanapaṇi)* ch. *Vastuna.*
22. *Ibid.*, No. 4, pp. 26-27.
23. *Ibid. Dāne surgō phlam samnṁ ™ praśr-sutsyochcheevrārchin ksutuati bhāsitm ™ ti-ni dim ch.... Bhallesvara gumine kāśyapaya dhuyrhe mahā-kumbhā rapadroko.*
24. *Ibid.*, pp. 36-40.
25. *Ibid.*

26. *Ibid.*, pp. 41-42, 16.
27. *Ibid.*, p. 50.
28. *EI*, IV, No. 34, pp. 243-45.
29. *Ibid.*, p. 255. These terms literary mean kings, ministers, chiefs of the armies, chief of the *viśayas* (or districts), chief of the *bhōga,* where the *bhōga* is perhaps equivalent to *bhukti,* denoting a larger extent of the territory than a *viśaya.*
30. *Ibid.*, p. 253, the term *śaśthādhikṛita* literary denotes a superintendent or comptroller of *Śaḍbhaga i.e.* 1/6 part of the produce, due to the king.
31. *Ibid.*, The term *khola* literary denotes a messenger.
32. *Ibid.*
33. *Jyetḥakāyośthas* means the chief writer.
34. The officers in charge of groups of ten villages.
35. *Ibid.*, p. 254. *Karaṇa* denotes a writer, scribe, accountant.
36. *Ibid.* The term *haṭṭika* might be described from *haṭṭa,* a market, and may mean market dues, and the term *talāvātaka* literary denotes the village accountant or land paying rent to the state.
37. *Ibid.*, p. 254.
38. *EI*, XVIII, No. 17, pp. 310-14.
39. *Ibid.*, 225. These villages were donated together the undivided lands attached to them, unbroken upto their boundaries, grass and pasture land, with their general places, mango and *madhūka* trees, with their water and dry lands, *uparikaras, daśaparādhas, chauroddaraṇas* free from all trouble.
40. *EI, XIX,* No. 2, p. 15.
41. *Ibid.*, p. 16.
42. *Ibid.*, p. 19.
43. *EI*, I, p. 97, II, pp. 482-83.
44. *Ibid.*, p. 107. A piece of land was donated by an inhabitant of kirāgrāma, named Geneśvara the son of the *Brāhmaṇa.*
45. *Ibid.*
46. *Ibid.*, Line - 34. A wealthy merchant named Jinaka, the son of Dipika and Malhika granted a piece of land to god 'Śiva' for the courtyard in front of temple.
47. *Ibid.*, p. 118. A piece of land to be cultivated by one plough and belonging to the village named Pralamba has been granted to Maheśa by Lakśana the mother of Rajnaka *"matra Rajamaka Lakśana ek-halayeneya-datta bhume meheśa-Laksana-mukkthḥ y. palyeyte tolnvydhtar.*
48. *Ibid.*, p. 115, Line-35. Whatever pious gift has thus been made by anybody for the sake of 'Śiva', may that last for his (benefit) as long as this earth exists.
49. *Ibid.*, p. 118, text, p. 115.
50. *Ibid. Bhumeya holctuṣ tyh yogyā dta mugrā mat* etc. *yi-na-yin- ydhtrukajḥ vehetḥ Śiva-smuddiṣya.*

51. Bhagwant Sahai, *The Inscription of Bihar,* Delhi, 1983, pp. 40-85, 75.
52. D.C. Sircar, *Select Inscription, op. cit.,* No. 15, pp. 668-69.
53. *EI,* XIV, No. 13, pp. 176-77.
54. *Ibid.*
55. *Ibid.*, p. 177.
56. *Ibid.*, pp. 180-81. It was probably a local dynasty of the Chahamanas which had entered into a subordinate alliance with king Bhoja Deva I, and helped him in his wars, thus giving the overlord great pleasure, Indra-raja built a temple for its upkeep.
57. *Ibid.*, p. 181.
58. *Ibid.*, p. 182.
59. *Ibid.* XXXVIII, No. 51, p. 289.
60. *Ibid.*, pp. 294-95.
61. *Ibid.*, p. 295.
62. *Ibid.*, p. 296.
63. *Ibid.*
64. *Ibid.*
65. *Ibid.*, p. 297.
66. *Ibid.*
67. *Ibid.*, pp. 297-98.

   "Sa-tala, Sōddēśa, S-āmsa-pañasa, sa-guvāka-nalikēra, sā-jala-sthala, sa-gort-ōśara-śa-jala-sthala, sa-gort-ośara-sa-das-āparādha-sā-chōr-*ōddhoraṇa, parilorita-sarva-pīda-a chāta bhāṭa pravśa, a kindid-grāhya, samasta-rājabhōga-Kāra-kiranya-viratyaya-sahita."*
68. K.K. Gopal, "Assignment to officers and Royal kinsmen in Early Medieval India", C.A.D. 700-1200, in B.P. Sahu (ed.), *LSRSEI, op. cit.*, p. 118. V.K. Thakur, *Historiography of Indian Feudalism; Towards a Model of Early Medieval Indian Economy,* Patna, 1989, p. 25. T. Watters, *On Yuan Chawang's Travels in India,* Vol. V, p. 176. Hiuen Tsang state that "those who are employed in Government services are paid according to their work. Minister of state and common officials all have their portion of land and are maintained by the cities assigned to them".
69. D.C. Sircar, *Landlordism and Tenancy, op. cit.*, p. 33.
70. *Ibid.*
71. *Ibid.*, pp. 33-34. Sircar argues that the donees of royal charters, who became landlords of the states granted to them, were not always *Brāhmaṇa* and temple authorities, and other persons, who sometimes succeeded in getting such estates created for them by making suitable payments of money to the king or as a result of service rendered to the state, belonged to different communities. He further argues that, in India, the king was never the actual owner of land under permanent tenants — but Sircar ignores all the 'facts regarding the king' ownership of land which are depicted in early Indian literary as well as epigraphical sources. He further argues that, 'the priestly class was the most unsuitable for rendering services of feudal type'.

He did not explain that how the priestly class is unsuitable for rendering services to the state. He states that the social position of the *Brāhmaṇa* donee was exceptionally high and he was not looked upon as the king vassal. But Sircar, does not throw proper light on the political and economic status of the *Brāhmaṇa* in early India who had played very important role in Ancient Indian Polity.

72. D.C. Sircar, cited in V.K. Thakur, *Historiography of Indian Feudalism, op. cit.*, pp. 25-26.
73. Om Parkash, *Early Indian Land Grants and State Economy,* Allahabad, 1988, p. 2. He argues that the nature of land-grants varied from region to region. The express characterisation of such charters as *karaśāśma* in these charters themselves, shows that a category of land-grants with a tax on it was absolutely tax-free while yet fixing a tax, and included even the imprecatory verses in a regular manner. Such land-grants are fairly widespread in time and space.
74. *Ibid.*, p. 3. Om Parkash argues that such grants possibly transferred, in effect, only the collection right along with the privileges and local taxes to the donees who were still obliged to pay the dues and taxes of central government than collected by them. He further argues that land-grants only contributed the kings share to the royal treasury but some of them also brought their prices to the king. A number of transaction though dressed in the form of land-grants were actually sold out to the donees. *Ibid.*, p. 4.
75. D.C. Sircar, *Landlordism and Tenancy..., op. cit.*, p. 49. And *El*, XXXI, pp. 281, 288, 296. Some documents include in the list such items as temples and ramparts and mine *(Khāni)* with special references to deposits of iron and other metals *(loh-ādy — ā kāra),* and sometimes also pits, road-crossing and barren spots as well as salt pits. Sometimes they include ponds (talla), tank, rivers and hills, the cows-huges, wood, bricks and stones, the dwellings of artisans, cultivators and traders, and domestic and wild animals and the birds and aquatic beings.
76. Om Parkash, *op. cit.,* p. 282. It has been argued that the practice of issuing tax free land-grants to *Brāhmaṇa* appears to have originated from the traditional precept of not only taxing the *Brāhmaṇa* but also providing the learned vedic scholars among them with their means of livelihood in form of plots of arable land exempt from all sorts of revenue demands. *Ibid.*, p. 283.
77. J.F. Fleet, *C1I,* III, No. 80, p. 286. D.C. Sircar, *Select Inscription, op. cit.,* No. 3, pp. 24-25, No. 4, 26, 27, *El,* IV No. 34, pp. 243-45, *El,* XVIII, No. 17, pp. 310-14. *E1*, XIX, No. 2, p. 15, *El,* XIX, No. 13, pp. 176, *E1*, XXXVII, No. 51, p. 289, *El,* XXI, pp. 281, 288, 296. Vogel, *Antiquities of Chamba State*, Part-l, pp. 167-69, *E1,* XXXII, pp. 122, 125, 217.
78. R.S. Sharma, *Indian Feudalism,* 2nd edition, Delhi, 1980, pp. 218-19. Sharma argues that "the land-grants may be regarded as an important factor in annexing new areas and new people to the caste system, which served to give some kind of uniform social order to the whole country. At the same

time such grants created new titles to revenues leading to the eventual fragmentation of political authority". *Ibid.*, p. 223.

79. Om Parkash, *op. cit.*, p. 283. "It as left no stone unturned to bring the rank and file of the *Brāhmaṇa* (who were mostly non-learned) into the actual network of taxation. On the normative plane as well, the *Mahābhārata,* sided with the state and openly that the Śūdra like *brāhmaṇa* should be taxed."
80. *Ibid.*, p. 287.
81. K.K. Gopal, in *CSRSEI, op. cit.*, p. 120.
82. *Ibid.*, pp. 127-28.
83. J.F. Fleet, *C11,* III, *op. cit.*, No. 80, p. 286.
84. *Ibid.*
85. D.C. Sircar, *Landlordism and Tenancy , op. cit.*, p. 35. Sircar, discusses that granting a village together with its inhabitants certainly does not refer to the king's or lord's proprietary right over the villagers. Because the donated land could be either inhabited or uninhabited, the grant of inhabited areas was sometimes stated to include the inhabitants (*i.e.* the right to collect taxes) etc. from them specifically.
86. *El,* III, p. 107. Sircar, *Landlordism and Tenancy, op. cit.*, p. 72.
87. *Ibid.*, p. 74 and Vogel, *Antiquities, op. cit.*, pp. 167-69. *El*, III, p. 107. *The Paithan Copper-plate Inscription,* records various exemptions to the donees. Such as (1) *S-odrañga* (together with the fixed or the taxes on permanent tenant), (2) *Sā-parikara* (Same as *S-oparikara,* together with occasional taxes or the taxes on temporary tenants), (3) *Sa-daś āparadha* (together with the power to deal with cases involving the ten officers, (4) *Sa-bhutapata pratyāya* (the same as *Sa-bhāt-opātta pratyāya* or *Sā-bhūt-vāta-pratyāya* together with the income resulting from earth quacks etc., together with the dues payable in kind and caṣh, free from the entry of a *cāṭa-bhaṭa* without the jurisdiction of any royal officer. An Inscription from *Chamba* records the following privileges (1) *Sua-sīmātrna-goyūthi-gocara-paryanta* (as far as its limits, grass and land, pound and pasture ground, (2) *Sa-vanaspaty vdak, āśithara-kullaka pāniya-sameta* (together with fruit trees and with various water courses and channels), (3) *S-āgami-nirgama-psaueśa* (with approaches ingress and egress), (4) *Sā-khila-potacya* (with fellow and cultivated land), (5) *Sā-daś-āparadha* (with fine for the ten officers), (6) *putrapartr-ādyanvay-opabhogyh* (to be enjoyed by succession of sons, grandsons and so forth), (7) *anācchedya* (uncurtailable), (8) a *paripanthya* (not to be opposed), (9) *a-cāṭa-bhaṭa-pravesa* (not to be entired by the *cāṭa* and *bhatas* of the collection of the taxes etc.) (10) a *kiñcit-kara* (fully free from taxes) and *anāhāra* (inalienation).
88. L. Gopal, *op. cit.*, pp. 249-52.
89. *Ibid.*, p. 253.

5

Formation of Agriculture in Early Medieval Northern India

The original meaning of the agriculture is the culture of soil (Latin, agricultural) but this is much too narrow an interpretation, the growing of crops and the rearing of livestock are as much part of agriculture as the original cultivation of the soil, though the latter is the first step in a chain of operations which provides foodstuffs for men, one simple definition of agriculture is the service and practice of farming, using the word in its broadest sense.

Our knowledge of agriculture is largely based upon information gained in the past by farmers by purely empirical means. Local practice is dependent upon a very careful marshalling of facts over a long period and the development of system which suits soil, climate or location.[1] However, the cultivation of the soil was one of the first forces in the development of civilization. It required that human beings stay in one place to care for the crops, instead of leading a wandering lives of hunters or shepherds. As people settled in small agricultural communities, they began to accumulate possessions and to adopt more socialized habits. Gradually, as more productive methods of agriculture were developed, and as knowledge spread, the increasing complexity of human relations led to the beginning of the great nations of the ancient world. The close connection between agriculture and civilization is illustrated by the fact that the early man's most important food crops, probably originated in the regions that were occupied by early cultures.[2]

The ancient synonym for agriculture is the Sanskrit term *kṛṣi,* derived from the word and *kṛṣi*, meaning 'to plough'.

Patanjali, argues the term *kṛṣi* in some broader sense. In his opinion, kṛṣi includes not only ploughing but also the feeding of ploughman, managing the seeds and bullocks and also doing subsidiary agricultural activities (like digging of land, sowing and reaping of crops, winnowing etc.). The economic life of early northern India was mainly agricultural, as it is even today. Agriculture has been playing a vital role in economic life of the early India, right from the remotest time. A large number of early Indian land-grants refer to the Agriculturists *kṛṣakah* or *kaṭumbinaḥ*, the members of the cultivating class. The cultivators were highly esteemed and their profession was an honourable one.

The word *Vārtā*[3] mentioned in *Arthaśāstra of Kauṭilya* and *kāmandakīyanitisara*[4] notices that the means of subsistence of *Vaiśya*, were cattle-rearing, cultivation and trade, and the occupation of those who lived by these means was called Vārāta. The *Vārāta* has been considered very important for the welfare of society. The *kāmandakīya-nitisāra* further argues that those who were proficient in *Vārāta* should be assured of freedom from want.[5] The *Sukra-nitīsāra*[6] gives a much more clear and sound definition of *Vārāta*, such as agriculture, commerce and cattle breeding. It seems that agriculture was one of the most important source of economic prosperity of the largest segment of population in early India, and the proper knowledge of agriculture was encouraged in ancient Indian society.

It has been argued that there was a great demand of land for cultivation and habitation. The cultivable and uncultivable land was brought under cultivation probably as a result of the gradual increase in population. Sometimes, even, the *Brāhmaṇa* and the *kṣatriyas* for whom agriculture was forbidden were permitted to adopt agriculture as their occupation in the times of emergency. Agriculture, as an occupation was prescribed for *Vaiśayas* by law givers but a large part of the *Śūdras* served as landless labourers. Thus, we observed that almost the people of all *Varṇas*, in some way or the other, were engaged in agriculture. The economy of the early northern India was agriculture centred or agrarian economy.

In early India the land was not allowed to remain fallow for an indefinite period, but other were prompted to make it productive, and for the encouragement of agricultural settlement the rulers donated quite large plots of cultivable land. These were revenue free royal donations, possible in view of the fact that the donee might be able to make land productive.[7] The establishment of irrigation works in many parts of early northern India, gave a further impetus to the growth of agriculture, even in the dry and barren lands. The land was gradually brought into cultivation,[8] by religious establishment. The bushes and jungles were cleared for cultivation, with the help of Iron implements and more and more land was brought under cultivation. The importance of agriculture was recognised in both religious as well as secular society during early Indian history.

It has been depicted in the inscription that the term *karṣatikārṣayati*,[9] means that it depend upon the *Brāhmaṇa* donee that whether he preferred cultivating the land by himself on get them cultivated by others. There is no indication that the donee could cultivate fields in emergency only. We notice that a large number of references to the *Brāhmaṇa* and the *kṣatriyas* engaged in cultivation.[10] Thus we can deduce that although lawgivers forbid two upper *Varṇas* from accepting agriculture as means of their livelihood, it affected only a small section of them who were piously devoted to their studies and enhancement of knowledge. In course of time due to increase in population and decrease in the popularity of the *yajñas*, it might have been realized that the ban on the *Brāhmaṇa* against cultivation was causing a hardship. A large number of them, however, could not bow down to these laws. As it can be proved, it was not always necessary to follow the rules laid down by these law regulations.[11]

The technique of forecasting weather involved the study of astronomy and was dependent on the experience and observation of natural phenomena accumulated over centuries till today. The *Kṛṣiparāśara*[12] of *Parāśara* mentions how the early Indian astronomers predicted monthly, yearly and immediate rainfall, the *Kṛṣiparāśara* further describes the rainfall in any year according to the planet who happen to be its king, minister or superintendent of water and crops. It shows that the astronomical predictions was the monopoly of *Brāhmaṇa* and the largest segment of the population was dependent on them for weather predictions.

In early India agriculture was largely conditioned by weather, including rainfall and the climatic factors also lent Indians to depend on agriculture. In early India the success of agriculture depended principally on the monsoon rains. We have noticed references to six seasons in epigraphical sources, and various term regarding the seasons are depicted in epigraphical records, such as, vasanta (spring), *grśma* (Summer), *Varṣa* (rainy), *Śarad* (autumn), hemanta (winter) and *śiṣira* (vernol autumn).[13] Dandin talks of the fundamental features of the seasons.[14] We do not find any variation in the phenomenal condition of early Northern India. The Western parts of the country were comparatively cold and dry than the eastern parts.[15] Alberuni argues that Multan had no *Varṣākāla*, as most of the Northern parts are near the mountains.[16] It shows that climatic factors played very vital role in the development of agriculture right from the very beginning, as the agriculture was the backbone of early Indian economy.

Early Indian literatures refer to the auspicious moments for commencing cultivation. The ploughing of the field was recommended under the constellations *mula*, *viśakha* and *Magha* and under mobile, fixed, slow and quick planets, or when the evil plants or stars were of weak influence, and the moon was in the mansion called *Jala* and visible in her full aspect. When the Jupiter was in *Lagna* mansion. It should not be done on Sunday and Saturday, nor at the time of Sun's entrance into Leo, Aquarians, Cancer, Aries, Capricorn, or Libra, for that causes emaciation of the body of the cultivators, nor on the fourth, sixth, ninth and fourteenth days of the lunar month called *Rīkta* (for the some season).[17] Muni Kaśyapa states in his work *Keśapina-kṛiṣi-sukti* that it is auspicious to cultivation when Jupiter is in lagna mansion, venus is strong, and the moon is in conjunction with *Purvasadha* when the evil stars are weak.[18] It shows that the peasants or cultivators kept in their minds various positions of the stars and plants while cultivating or sowing or harvesting the crops.

The classification of land is suggested by early Indian sources, described, as the types of land, *viz.*, arid, wet and moderate. *Kṛṣi-sukti* a comprehensive book on "Agriculture Science" attributed to Kaśyapa classified the land such as, (a) wet lands for paddy fields, named variously *Shuli Bhūmi, Jala Bhūmi* and *Sasya*

Bhūmi and (b) Dry land called *Adhaka bhūmi, Tara Bhūmi* and *Usva Bhūmi.*[19] He further classified land according to their suitability for particular crops.[20] We notice that sometimes soils were differentiated on the basis of colours.[21] Some literary works classified land after taking into account various kinds of crops grown upon them.[22] Many land-grants found throughout early northern India which refer the term like, *sajala-sthala*, *Śagartoṣaraḥ*, *Salohelavaṇā karaḥ*; *sonanavaṭikātaḍāga*, *sajhātanatapa yuti*, *sarvnasaneksu — karpasa — kusuma vṛhikṣetra* and *godhūmuā pakskakṣetra*,[23] these terms give the description of special features of the soil and the classification of soil or quality of soil and its use. It was the realization that the field near rivers are more fertile which must have led people to attach importance to them.[24] *Medhatithi* argues about the knowledge of the qualities of the soil and explains *uṣara*[25] as that part of the land where, on account of the defects of the soil, seeds do not spring.

Tillage implements. The culture of land is the first and foremost operation in agricultural production. This consist in breaking up the lumps of earth and smoothing and leveling prior to sowing of seed so as to bring about improvement in physical condition of the soil conducive to the healthy growth of the crops.[26] The *Paraśara* suggests the need for proper implements and argues that they must be strong and sound, otherwise agriculturists may face trouble at each step.[27] The plough happened to be the implement utilised for such purposes from the dawn of civilization, the plough and lute seem to be the two symbols of cultural evolution of humanity.[28]

The material and the aesthetic. The importance of the plough is described in the *Kṛṣiparāśara* and different parts of the plough and their measurements are mentioned. According to the *Parāśara,* "the plough consists essentially of eight parts; such as, Isa (the pole of the plough), *yuga* (the yoke), *niryola* (the rod of the plough exclusive of the pole and the share), *Niryolapaśika* (Iron plates that fix the share to the Niryola)."[29] There are two pairs of *Paśika*, *Halashthonu* (a strong piece of wood that is fixed to the *Niryola* at the end opposite to when the plough share is fixed; this is held by the cultivator while ploughing the field), *Addacalla* (the pins of yoke where the bullocks are tied), *Savla* (an extra piece of wood that tightly fixes the *Niryola* to the pole) and *Paccani*[30] (good). The *Abhidhānratramālā* of Halayudha discusses about the measurement of the plough parts, Isa is five cubits long, Sthanu two and half cubits, *niryola* one and half cubits,[31] *Paccani* is made of bamboo with Iron-top and about three or four and half-feet long "*Abandha* (a rod of Iron which presents the *niryola* from getting out of the pole) must be cylindrical and about one foot long, *yoktra*, four cubits in length, a rope five cubits in length, a rope five cubits long and *phala* (plough share) one cubitor *i.e.*, one cubit and four inches.[32] It seems that the construction of a plough handily differed from what it is in the present days use. Some other important implements for agricultural purposes are mentioned in *Abhidhānaratramālā* of Halayudha and *Abhidhānaratramālā* of Hemachandra such as spades (*godannam* or *kuodala*), goads (*pratodah*, *trotram, Lunaṃ* etc.), Sickle (*dātramlavitram*), hols, *khanitram*, *avadāraṇam*.[33] The sickle had a wooden handle for the convenience of being caught by the hand.[34] It shows that the sickle was just like that of a modern days sickle.

The kṛṣi-Parāśara[35] records a detailed account of how and when the plough should be put into operation. The first plying of plough should be done the *Svati, Uttara-rohini Mrgsiras, Mula Punarvash, Pusya, Sravana* and *Hasta* constellations. The peasants should start the working of the plough on Fridays, Mondays, Tuesdays and particularly on Wednesdays for the increase of their happiness. The beginning of cultivation on Tuesdays, Sundays, the tenth, and eleventh, the second and fifth, the thirteenth, the third and the seventh days of lunar are good for the commencement of cultivation.[36] Pārāśara further suggests that the plying of the plough should always be done when the sun is in the Taurus, pisces, virgo, Gemini, or the scorpio sign. Plying of the plough, when the sun is in the Aries kills the cattle, when in the Cancer, there is danger from water, when in the Leo, there is the fear of Snakes and when in the Aquarius, that the thieves.[37] In the sign capricornus, the sun destroys the crops and in the Libra, it causes danger of life. Hence, one should always take great care in selecting the movement of the sun's entrance into a zodiacal sign at the commencement of ploughing.[38] Ploughing being the first process in cultivation naturally receives careful attention from a cultivator. The *Kṛṣiparāśara* lays down the performance of ceremony called *halaprasāraṇa*[39] before the performance of ploughing and observes that he who starts cultivation without performing *Lalaprasāraṇa* does it in vain. The *Abhidhāna Ratnamāla* and *abhidhāna Chintamaṇi* suggest that land should be ploughed several times, not less than twice.[40]

Early Indian agriculture rested on irrigation and natural rain. Irrigation occupied a prominent position in the agriculture of India right from the earliest time, and it had played an important role in the agricultural industry of early India. Over a large part of the country rain has always been unequally and irregularly distributed and that is why, we find that from very early times, Indian peasants or cultivators and have sought to supplement the rainfall by digging well and censer it by tanks and storage reservoirs wideners, both literary and epigraphical have been given to show that great solicitude was displayed for irrigation in the past. The *Ṛgveda* contains references to the well-being used for watering the field. The word *Avata* means a well. We came to know from the later vedic literature and Buddhist texts that water was powered into channel and set to different part of the field.[41] The archaeological evidences tell us that a channel and dockyard with embankment walls, built out of burnt brisks uneartheathed at Lothal dated 1500 B.C. to 1000 B.C.[42] In *Arthaśāstra* irrigation is discussed in detail and lays down that irrigation tax (*Urḍh-bhāgha*)[43] should be given to the state by the peasants. Manu states that the boundary of the field should be determined by tanks, ponds, channels and other reservoirs of water.[44] The Junagarh Rock Inscription of Rudradamn[45] records how the Sudarjana lake was originally excavated by Chandragupta Maurya with the help of the *Vaiśya* and got repaired from time to time even the same lake rebuilt by Chakarapalita governor of Skandragupta.[46] But we notice in *Bṛhaspatismṛti* that irrigation had become a local responsibility but not a state affairs. After a critical study of the contents of the land-grants,[47] we find that literary sources, the importance of irrigation was recognised during the time of draught and shows that priority was given to irrigation by the state and the people alike in actual practice. Land-grant refers to the term *Jalakara* meaning irrigation tax.[48] *Rājatarangiṇi* of Kalhana mentions that Lalitaditya a king of Kashmir constructing a large number of water-wheels and distributed them to various villages.[49] The Aparajitāpṛccha[50] tells about strong machines to wells, and *abhidhānaratnamālā* describes the term araghattaka,[51] as a wheel on machine for lifting water from wells. The another literary source *upamitibharapranñcākathā* refers to the term araghaṭṭa.[52] Some of the land-grants refer the term *aryhaṭa* or *arhata* as an object of gift[53] and sometimes in connection with the enumeration of boundaries.[54] It shows that the arghata was not within the reach of a common peasant. The *Partabgarh* inscription that these might have been owned by kings, feudal lords, ministers and opulent merchant.[55]

We notice that during our period of study there was the growth in claims and power of state to establish their ownership over irrigational water, but several land-grants depict the donee's ownership of water.[56] It seems that all the wells, tanks and ponds etc. in the village were not owned by the state. It is clear that the man who had a well dug on his own land was its natural owner.[57] Which shows that all there irrigational activity in early Indian history might affect the ultimate dependence of early Indian agriculture on the rain.[58]

From the earliest times, rice, wheat and millets have been staple food of the largest segment of population in early India. In addition to these, references are abundant in ancient literature about the existence and usage of several other crops of economic importance such as sugarcane, barley, mango, Jute, ginger, turmeric, pumpkin, gourd, cucumber, pepper, mustard, cabbage, potato, radish, peas, kalai (pulses) etc. From the modern point of view, it is seen that different varieties or strains of a particular crop have to be evolved either by breeding or by selection to suit a particular type of soil and climate. Considering the wide diversity in soil and climate found in early northern India, it is expected to find a large number of varieties of crop.

The *Rāmacharita* and *Rājatarangiṇi*[59] use of term *Dhānya* for rice or paddy crops and same is the case with term *Vṛhi*. Kalhana mentions that during the time of famine *khāri* of *dhānya* was sold at very high prices.[62] Rice was grown throughout the year and based on the harvesting season they have classified in four main groups, *viz. Grishmika,* the summer; *Varshika*, the rainy, *Sarada*, the autumn; and *haimana* the winter. In all the countries, such as, Kashmir, Bengal, Kosala, Kura, Sindhlu-Sanvira (Sind and neighbourhood of Indus), Sura Sena (Mathura), cultivation was advisable in time when there was rainfall.[61] We find three kinds of rice in ancient India, based on their flavour and colour. They are *Śāli, Kalamā* and *sastika*, of them *kalamā* rice was somewhat hard and bright and possessed great flavour. But *Sastika* rice was without any flavour, and śāli was declared to be twenty-six varieties according to the various countries and the soil in which it is produced.[62] We notice twenty-one variety of rice in the work of a Muslim Writer[63] and the *Mānasollāsa*[64] refers eight varieties and five by Medhatithi. The *Abhidhānachintamaṇi*[65] of Hemachandra refers seventeen varieties of rice.[66] Some of the Inscriptions of early Indian history provide information regarding the cultivation of rice on large scale.[67] It is very clean from literary as well as epigraphical sources, that right from the vedic period down to the present days, rice was the chief crop grown in northern India throughout its length and breadth.

The next important crop was wheat. Some literary as well as epigraphical sources provide information regarding cultivation of wheat.[68] These sources indicated that the Punjab, Uttar Pradesh, Rajasthan and Sindh were great wheat producing areas.[69] The cotton constituted another important commercial product of the northern India. The qualities and textures of cotton differed according to the places where they were grown.[70] The *Manāsollāsa* discusses the features of the cotton grown in the different places.[71] We notice from the work of the foreign travellers, that the northern India was the major cotton growing centres.[72] We observe from the *Saduktikarṇāmṛta* that the cotton was obtained from the tree called *Śālamali* and seems that it was product of a every village in northern parts of India.[73] It shows that cotton was an important product of India from earliest times to the present days. The use of cotton in manufacturing clothes was known in the period of Indus-valley culture. Weaving was a common industry among the Ṛgvedic Āryas.[74] It shows that cotton has been used as an item of trade right from the remotest time to the present days.

Sugarcane was always been a very famous product of Northern India. References to Sugarcane (*Iksudanda*) and its several varieties has been mentioned in various sources of early India.[75] The *kāvgaṃimāsā* refers the kāśakāra and the *puṇḍra* varieties of sugarcane,[76] and the cultivation of sugarcane is indicated in the *Naiṣadhīyacharitam*,[77] *Poṇḍa* variety sugarcane is depicted by Barani and other Muslim writers, that Sind[78] was the main area of sugarcane cultivation. It is depicted in the *Rājatarangiṇi* that Kashmir also produce Sugarcane.[79] The *Rāmacharitya* refers to the cultivation of sugarcane plant in Varendri,[80] Some inscriptions speak of it as an important product of early northern india.[81] It is very clean from the literary as well as *epigraphical* sources that Northern India was the most important region for its cultivation.[82] Oilseeds of various kinds were known and cultivated in different regions of India. Some inscription of early northern India refer to oil seeds (*Sarshapa yānaka*) and oilmills (*tilapiḍana-yantra*).[83] These oil men and oil-mills were sometimes subjected to the payment in kind of a rent, as depicted in a few inscriptions.[84] *Yava* or barley was another grain and closely connected with black hair of barley. Corns are[85] described in the *Śiśira* season. Medhatithi also speak of yava.[86]

We have ample references to pulses, *mudga* (both black and yellow varieties)[87], *katāya* (pea, chanka, or chick pea), *kulatha* (horse grain), *masūra*, valla, *āḍhakī*, maṣa and *rājamāṣa* have been mentioned in *Abhidhānaratnamālā* of Kattanimata,[88] *Rājatarangiṇi*[89] and *Mānasollāsa* of Someśvara speak of seven varieties of beans.[90] Some inscriptions of early northern India also refer to various varieties of pulses.[91]

For the cultivation of vegetables Kaśyapa suggests that farmers should cultivate delicious vegetables like *Jatika Rasijatika, Valhika, Vana-Vallika, Patolika, Sanaka,* pumpkin, gourd, *kalata, kustumburn, surana, sakata, haldi* and ginger etc.[92] Various kinds of '*sāga*' are mentioned by Muslim writers,[93] even inscription supports that lotus roots were eaten by the *saina* saint and refer to certain vegetable, *e.g. alābh, kusmāṇḍa-Vallarin* and *Śākapatra.*[94] The forest yielded a large variety of edible fruits — mango, pomegranate, Jaok, banana, date, *vilva, kapitha*, rose-apple, coconut, palm-vines, etc.[95] were specially grown in Punjab and the North-West Frontiers. The *Rāmacharita* speaks of various trees such as, *aśoka, amalaka, karuna, pariyola*, etc.[96] The agriculture has been the main occupation of largest segment of ancient Indian society. Two of the most important sections of *vārtā* were agriculture and cattle-rearing, including dairy farming under the latter. The importance attached to agricultural pursuits by our economists is shown by the injunctions to kinds to study *vārtā*, and by the precept that a considerable part of the king is own revenue should be derived, both directly and indirectly, from the proceeds of agriculture and the rearing of cattle.[97] The agriculture was prescribed for *vaiśyas*, and *śūdras*, others were also permitted to agriculture.[98] Even a Brāhmaṇ could take to agriculture.[99] Well to do *Brāhmaṇas* were given useful employment in the backward, aboriginal tracts where they could spread new methods of cultivation. Some beliefs and rituals sponsored by the priest helped material progress among the tribal people.[100] Since then, the killing of cow was considered as bad as homicide helped towards the preservation of cattle wealth, so essential for agriculture. The priest taught the primitive people not only the use of the plough and manure but also fostered agriculture by giving them the knowledge of seasons and planets, especially of the recurrence of the rain.[101] One of the most technical work on agriculture is *kṛṣi-parāśara*. The land-grants provided the administrative mechanism for maintaining law and order in the donated area, in which all such powers were delegated to the donees.[102] The largest part of the ancient Indian state's income probably came from land revenue.[103] Waste lands were to be brought under cultivation; jungle was to be cleared,[104] it seems to be the direct impact of issuance of widespread of land-grants. It has been argued that the fertilisers are to be used, local markets are to be founded for the exchange of agricultural produce. The productivity of a piece of land is dependent not merely on its soil, irrigability and cultivability, but on its quality of extensions, size, situation and accessibility.[105]

After long survey of literary and epigraphic sources we could be able to deduce that the agrarian growth and rural expansion was an important phenomenon in early Indian history. The patronage extended by the kings, feudal lords to agriculture, improvement in irrigational facilities, increasing knowledge of agricultural sciences etc. were some of the connotative factors which strengthened rural economy. Decline of towns may have led to the migration of a number of skilled artisans into the countryside. Some of them changed their profession and adopted agriculture as their profession in villages which stimulated agrarian growth.

REFERENCES

1. S.J.W., *Agriculture in Chambers' Encyclopaedia*, published by George Newnes Limited, London, 1950, p. 157.
2. Thatcher (ed.), *The Universal World Reference Encyclopaedia*, Chicago, 1962, p. 125.
3. *Pātanjali*, III, 1.26 *Aś* 4, p. 8.
4. *Kāmandakīyanistīśāra* (ed.) Vidya Sagara, J.P. Calcutta, 1875, Tr. Dutta, M.N., Calcutta, 1896, II. 20.
5. *Ibid.,* II.14.
6. B.K. Sarkar (Jr.), *Śukra-nitīsāra*, Allahabad, 1914. 1, 311-12.
7. S.K. Maity, *Economic Life of Northern India in the Gupta Period*, Calcutta, 1957, pp. 71-72.
8. *Ibid.*, p. 72.
9. *EI*, XXVII, No. 37, p. 201, 1.20. *EI*, II, No. 15, p. 220, II 87-88.
10. *Kathākaśaparakaraṇa* Introduction, pp. 119-20, tent, pp. 113-14. Padma Purāṇa, pt. II, p. 371 Slokas 6-8.

    G.V. Acharya, *Historical Inscription of Gujrata*, III, p. 200. *EI*, I, p. 184, Footnotes.
11. S.M. Devi, *op. cit.*, pp. 3-4.
12. G.P. Majumdar and S.C. Banerji (eds.), *The kṛṣiparāśara of parāśara,* Calcutta, 1960, Vol. 10.
13. *EI*, XX No. 13, 1.5.
14. *Dvyaśrayakāvya Dandin,* Ch. III, VV, 167-68.
15. S.M. Devi, *op. cit.*, p. 7.
16. E.C. Sachar (ed.), *Kitab-ul-hind*. (Albereni's India) Vol. 1, pp. 211-12. London, 1910, Vol. I, pp. 211-12.
17. *Bṛaht-Parāśara*, cited in *Agriculture in Ancient India*, published by Indian Council of Agricultural Research, Delhi, 1964, p. 110. It has been suggested that "one should begin ploughing under the nineteen constellations comprising *Mula visakha* and *Magha* along with the mobile, fixed, slow and fast constellations. The first ploughing with the ball should be done under the constellations that are slow, fixed, fast and mobile as well as under *viṣakha* and those saved to the pitṛs.
18. *Ibid.*, p. III. Kaśyapa says, "If meditary on *Śitā*, sowing is done under *punaravaṣa Svati, Mula*, and under the constellations that are fast, fixed and slow, it yield rich harvest." As regards the influence of the Zoological

cycle on ploughing, Kaśyapa says, "There eight, nine and seven constellations beginning from the one list by the sun cause loss, gain, death of the cultivator and the acquisition of wealth respectively." *Ibid.*, pp. 111-12.

19. *Ibid.*, p. 6. The nine kinds of *Jāti, Śri-Sandika* (Sandaltree), *Ketaki* (*Padanus odoratissi news*), *Ketaka*? *Amba, Kakaca, urdivi,* rose-apple and other similar, trees and plants grow in mash land. The cultivated tree like the *Campaka Patala*, mango, Bakula, should be planted in a moderate land. Trees, plants, and creepers which grow best on acid land neene *Dhava, Khadira, Vamsa Sina tara*, etc., *Ibid.*, p. 7.
20. *Ibid.*, p. 9. *Kaśyapa* is of the view that neither avoid nor west land is good. It is the moderate land which is neither too wet nor to dry, on which, all kinds of trees can grow. *Ibid.*, p. 10.
21. *The Aufrecht* (ed.), *Abhidhānarathnanīda* of Halyaha, Lahore, 1928, 11.5.
22. H.D. Bechar Das and Muni Jinavijayji (ed.), *Abhidhānachintamaṇi* of *Hemachandra*, Bhavanagar, 1914-19-iv 31-33, *Abhidhānaratnamālā* ii. 7.9, *Manu* ix, 39, *Medhatithi* and *Kullaka* on *Manu*, ix, 36-40.
23. *EI*, xiv, No. 23, p. 327, 1.43. *E1*, iv, No. 20, p. 157, 1. 117. *E1*, x 11, No. 10, p. 53, 1159-60, *E1*, 11, p. 240, 1.56.
24. L. Gopal, *The Economic Life, op. cit.*, p. 297.
25. Medhatithi's *Commentary on Manu*, 11, 12.
26. *Agriculture in Ancient India*, *op. cit.*, p. 34.
27. *Kṛṣiparāśara*, V.V. 119-20.
28. *Ibid.*
29. *Ibid.*
30. *Bṛhat-parāśara* in *Dharmaśāstra Saṅgraha* (ed.), Jivananda, Vidya Sagara Bhattacharya, Calcutta, 1876, 11, p. 107.
31. *Ibid.*
32. *Ibid.*, *Abhidhānaratnamālā, op. cit.,* vv. 577. L. Gopal discusses the various parts of plough and its size such as *Yuga* (Yoke) which is mentioned as extending upto cows of the oxen, 2. *addacalla* on the pin of the yoke where is bullocks are tied with measure 12 *angulas* (9 inches), 3. Yotra on yoke tie which is to be 4 hastas (6 feet), 4. raffu on string, 5. Isa on the pole of the rod of the plough to be 5 hastas (7 feet 6 inches), long, 6. *niryola* on the rod of the plough exclusive of the pole and the share measuring of the pole and the share measuring 1 *hasta* (2 feet 3 inches)..., 10. *phala* on plough share which is one *hasta* and 5 *angulas,* 11. *halasthana* the handle of the plough or a piece of wood fixed to the *niryola* at the end opposite to which the cultivator holds while ploughing. L. Gopal, *Economic Life, op. cit.,* p. 305. Plough was for the most important implement for which terms, like, *hala*, *langala*, *phala*, *Kusika*, *godarana* have been given in literary sources and Inscription.... The terms like *Isa nirisa, Kutakam-phala* have been mentioned. An inscription, refers to term like *halaukuṭaka* and *halakheṭala*, perhaps meaning a ploughman. S.M. Devi, *Economic Condition, op. cit.,* pp. 12-13.

33. *Abhi, Ratna, op. cit.*, 11, 421, *Abhichint, op. cit.*, 111.556.
34. *Abi-chint, 111.*
35. *Ibid.*
36. *Agriculture in Ancient India, op. cit.*, p. 40.
37. *Ibid.*
38. *Ibid.*
39. *Kṛṣpārśara, v.v.* 121-56.
40. *Abhi-mālā* 11,421; *Abhi-Chinti,* 111, 556, Iv, 34. S.M. Devi, is of the opinion that there is also referred in the lexicons and other literature of land being ploughed several times, not less than twice, as the phrase *Sambarkrit* (ploughing twice) suggests. Sometimes, *dvihalya*, and *trsitya* also occur, such is the method still followed by the agriculturist when dry, the field was most probably ploughed once as is done these days. The clods mere than broken by means of the method of *lostabhedana* (*Kotisah Langa)* and the field-reploughed for the second time in the wet condition and made even by the application of *lostabhedana* (*matyam, samikaranm tatra, op. cit.*, p. 24.
41. *Ṛgveda* 1.85.10, 1.660.0, IV 17.16, VIII, 49.6. X25.4 Ar. Veda 1.64, XIX 2.2. *Kansika-Sūtra*, 40.1.10. *Bodhayāna*, 11.3.5, 5-6. Panino, III, 123.
42. *Indian Archeological : A Reveiw,* 1958-59, p. 14 (IAR).
43. *Aś* 11.1, 111, 9.
44. *Manu Smṛti*, VIII, 248.
45. *EI*, VIII, No. 6, 35.
46. *Ibid.*, XVI, p. 235.
47. *Ibid.*, XVI, p. 235. *Bṛ Smṛti*, XVII, 11-12.
48. *EI*, XX, No. 13, C11, IV, p. 86, 1.28 (*Vāpi-kupataḍāga*) M.A. Stein (ed.), *Rājatarangiṇi* of Kalhana, Westminster, 1900, IV, 191, V 68-121,
49. *EI*, XII, p. 219, VIII, p. 158, p. 120, X, p. 99.
50. *Rāj*. IX-191.
51. *Aparajita prccha of Bhuvandeva* (ed.), P.A. Mankad, Baroda, 1950, p. 274.
52. *Abhi-Mālā*-VI, 685. L. Gopal, *Aspects of History of Agriculture in Ancient India*, Varanasi, 1980, pp. 114-68.
53. P. Peterson, *Upamitibhavaprapañcā kathā of Siddharsi*, Calcutta, 1899, pp. 66. 418, 418, 723.
54. *EI*, XIV, 186, 1.26.
55. *EI*, XI, p. 28, CII, IV, 324-31.
56. *EI*, XIV, p. 182.
57. *EI*, XIV, 186, 1,24, XV, 295, XXVIII, 327-28, CII, IV, 324-31.
58. M.N. Dutt (Tr), *Agnipurāṇa*, Calcutta, 1903, CCLVII, "Bhattasuamin is of the view that those well versed in the *śāstras* view the king as the owner of the land and water. But in ancient India the state never thought of

deriving any income from its ownership of Irrigation works. It was regarded as a pious duty on the part of king to provide such work of public utility. However, the many demands on the purse of the feudal state led it in its desire to tap new sources of revenue, to utilise its ownership of irrigational works as a separate source of income", L. Gopal, *Economic Life...*, *op. cit*. pp. 291-92.

59. R.C. Majumdar, R.G. Basak (eds.), *Rāmacharita of Sandhyākaranandi*, Rajashahi, 1939, 111, 17.
60. *Rāj*., V. 71.
61. *Ibid*., V. 71, 271.
62. A.A.I., pp. 59-60.
63. *Ibid*., p. 62. "The 23 varieties of Soli rice are (1) White soli (2) Red Soli (3) Thick Soli (4) Long *Sali*, having sweet flavour (5) White Coloured *Kalma* (6) *Sambaka* rice called *hema*, golden (7) Reddish brown Sambaka (8) Red-*Sambaka* (9) black *Samba*, another varieties considered to be very flavoury (10) *Suka* rice (11) another thick variety of Urihi (12) *Hard Vrihi* (13) *Palasa Vrihi* which was full of flavour (14) *Svadu vrihi* which was very swet (15) *Phala Vrihi* (16) *Draksa* (grape) *Vrihi* (17) *Nivana* which had black and white spots (18-19) white *yava* and black *yava* bot of which are thick (20) *Sammar vrihi* which had on abundant crop or swells much on boiling (21) *kala vrihi* which was very nourishing (22) white *Vrihi* and (23) yellow vrihi which removes indigestion." *Ibid*. and S.M. Devi, *op. cit*., p. 20.
64. *IHQ* XXVII, p. 193 footnote.
65. G.K. Śhrigonadakar (ed.), *Mānasottāsa* of *Someśvara*, XXVII and LUXXXIC, III, 1346-48, 1359.
66. Medhatithi on *Manu*, VIII, 320. Among the food grains, rice of several varieties were mentioned. *Śāli* was considered to be a fine variety of rice, such as *Salih, raktsalih, mahasalih, mahāśalih* and *kalāmah*. *Śālikanda* and *Selichurna* and red were was mentioned. S.M. Devi, *op. cit*., p. 19.
67. *Abhi-māni*, *op. cit*., IV, 233. Pushpa Niyogi argues that the word *dhanya* is used by Hemachandra in a wider sense and signifies grains in general and not merely rice. Thus, *vrihi, yava, masura, godhuman* (wheat), *mudga* (*green gram-hinid-murg-pulse*), *masha* (black gram), tila, (Sesame), *Chanaka* (Bengal gram) is commonly used as fodder, for horses, *anava* (the meaning of the word is not clear), Pushpa Niyogi, *op. cit*., p. 23.
68. *El*, XXI, pp. 42. *El*, I, 287, footnotes IA. XVI, p. 7. *Chaumola copper-plate inscription of somavarme deva and Asatadeva*, *El*, XI, the *Bhinmal stone inscription of Udayasimha of the Chahamana dynasty*.
69. Niyatakālakaṇḍa of Lakhsmidhara, 396-97; kṛtgaratnākara, pp. 257-78. H.M. Elliot, J. Dowson (eds.), *History of India as told by its own Historian*, Vol. I, London, 1866-67, pp. 15-16. *El*, II, p. 236, XI, p. 55, footnotes, X, p. 57 (*Bhinamala Inscription*).
70. S.M. Devi, *op. cit*., p. 38.
71. *Mānasollāsa*, III, 1017-20.

72. S.S. Nadvi, *Arab-aur-bhārata ke sambandha*, Allahabad, 1930, p. 25. A. Ricci (Tr), *The Travels of Marcopolo*, London, 1950, 3rd impression, 11.393, 115. S.M. Devi, argues that during the period of the paramaras, Ujjain was a centre of textile industry, and shepherad's colony in Ujjain is referred, and it appears that the cotton was ordinary product of the Chandella kingdom, and toll on a article of trade during Paramar rule, S.M. Devi, *op. cit.*, p. 39.
73. *Saduktikarṇāmṛta of Śrīdharadasa,* (ed.) R. Sharma, Lahore, 1933, IV, 55.1-5.
74. P. Niyogi, *Contribution of the Economic History*, *op. cit.*, pp. 27-28.
75. B. Kunjalal (tr), *Suśrutasamḥita*, 3 volumes, Calcutta, 1907, 45, 138-40.
76. Medhatithi *on Manu*, VIII, 326. C.D. Dalal R.A. Sastri (ed.), *Kāvya mimamsa of Rajaśekhara*, 3rd edition; A Baroda, 1939. XII.
77. *Naiṣadhiyācharitam of Śrīhara*, (tr) K.K. Handique, Lahore, 1934, XXI, 153, VIII, 2 sloke 101.
78. *HIED, op. cit.* I, pp. 15-16, 24, 27-28, 35, 37-40, 81.
79. *Rāj*. 11.60, VII, 1574.
80. *Rāmacharity*, V. 17.b, p. 71.
81. *EI*, XVI, pp. 272, p. 131, I.A. XXV, p. 205, ff. XVI, p. 208. *E1*, XIV, p. 300.
82. Sir G. Watt, *Dictionary of the Economic Products of India* (in six volumes), London, 1891, Vol. VI, p. 58 ff.
83. *E1*, XVIII, p. 60. *E1*. I, p. 97.
84. *EI*, I, p. 287, XIV, p. 176, I.A. XLI, p. 5.
85. *E1*, XI, p. 46, *Saduktikarṇāmrta* II, 136.5.
86. *Medhatithi on Manu*, VIII, 320.
87. *Abhi Māla*, II, 425-29, 110.
88. *Kuṭṭanimatam of Damodargupta,* (tr) Atrideva Vidyalankara, Varanasi, 1961, *Śloka*, 229.
89. *Rāj*. VII. 758.
90. *Mānasollāsa*, III, pp. 1346-48, B. 58.
91. *E1*, XI, p. 56 ff.
92. *Agriculture in Ancient India*, *op. cit.*, p. 72, *Raj*. VIII 676, V, 676, VIII, 134, 143.
93. S.M. Devi, *op. cit.*, pp. 25-26.
94. *E1*, I, *Deopara Inscription*, II, 21-22, V. 23, *E1*, XXI, No. 23, 1.15.
95. *HIED*, I, pp. 39-67, *Ramacharity*, V, p. 93.
96. *Rāmacharity*, V, p. 90.
97. K.V. Rangaswami, *Aspects of Ancient Indian Economic Thought*, Banaras, 1934.
98. *Ibid*. It shows that the agrarian growth expanded in early India another discusses the agricultural pursuits in Ancient India. Such matters as irrigation

by rain, rivers, channels, tanks and mechanical agencies, agricultural drainage, the use of fertilisers, the rotation of crops, the adjustment of crops to soils and the modification of soils to suit crops, the relative benefits of intensive and extensive cultivation, the value of even inferior. *Ibid.*, p. 78. Land in the vicinity of centres of population.

99. B.K. Sarkar (Tr), *Śukraniti-sāra*; 1914.
Jibānada (ed.), Sukraniti-Sara, with Commentary, 1890.
100. R.S. Sharma, *Indian Feudalism*, *op. cit.*, p. 222.
101. *Ibid.*
102. *Ibid.*
103. K.V. Rangaswami, *op. cit.*, p. 78. It has been argued that "the ancient Indian administrators and economists advocated the uninterrupted pursuit of agriculture even in the times of war...for the purpose of maintaining intact the existing irrational facilities, a joint and several liability is imposed upon the members of a village for keeping their roads, water channels and tanks in efficient repair." *Ibid.*, pp. 78-82.
104. *Ibid.*, p. 80.
105. *Ibid.*, p. 81.

The agrarian expansion can be seen in the *Bṛihat samḥita Agni purāṇa kṛṣarāśara*. The *Harṣacharita* speaks about different type of cultivation : plough cultivation, spade cultivation and slash and burn cultivation. The *kaśyapiakṛsisukti*, deals with all aspects of agriculture at length.

6

Conclusion

In conclusion, it can be safely surmised from this detailed study and evaluation of one of the most critical period of early medieval history, no doubt, vouched on agrarian expansion, but it left the peasantry on easy prey to the conquerors of medieval North India. Though it resulted in polarization of *varṇas*, yet it left them as 'cannon fodder' in modern parlance. The study, therefore, present a deteriorating grim scenario, about the socio-economic condition of the historical period spanning from 8th century to 10th century A.D. it also traces the causal complexities which forced the peasant to accept their fate passively and without a murmur.

The archaeological sources relating to Harṣa period are suggesting agrarian growth and rural expansion on an unprecedented scale. The patronage provided by the states, princes and chief to agriculture to improvement in irrigation facilities, to increasing knowledge of agricultural sciences etc. were some of the causative circumstances which strengthened rural economy. Urban decay led to the migration of a number of skilled artisans into the countryside. Some of them even changed their vocations which resulted in the dispersal of technical skill along with artisans and craftsmen into the countryside and stimulated agrarian growth and therefore, these skilled artisans adopted non-productive works like, snake charming, flute playing and jugglery. Land-grants in tribal frontiers brought virgin land under cultivation.

Therefore, this study traces the evolution of early medieval Indian agrarian expansion chiefly between the period from 8th century A.D., and concludes with the Turkish raids in northern India in the 10th century A.D., which in turn signalled the beginning of early medieval period at best, covered fragmentarily in the existing socio-economic literature. This period of early medieval Indian History saw rise and the growth of agrarian formation, and reflected the history of bitter feudal conflict between the peasants and feudal lords. It does not throws light not only on ignorance, religious fanaticism, and feudal brutality but also on agrarian formation and feudal economy.

No doubt, innumerable studies of peasantry have been made by historians, anthropologists, sociologists and other scholars, yet it is very difficult to group this class as one "-ism" like capitalism, socialism and feudalism, etc. because "peasantry" has been very volatile throughout the history of mankind. Thus, word peasant which otherwise stands for an individual assumes micro level meaning when put together as "peasantry", as it transgresses all boundaries of all states and comes to encompass all classes of the world. Hence, I have found it very difficult to categorize "peasant".

Hence, the study of the socio-economic formation of early medieval India engages the attention of the scholars of the day. It continues to baffle them. I have tried to find an improbable possible solution of this malady. This study also highlight the agrarian aspect of feudal system in early medieval India, which ultimately resulted in the transformation of Śūdras in to peasants. It seems that in the older settled regions Śūdras were provided with land rights in remote parts the tribal areas and the peasantry was annexed to the Brāhmaṇical system through land-grants. Some of the charters clearly show that the peasants, villages, and other inhabitants of the donated villages invariably carried out the orders of the donee?

Economic history describes man's efforts to satisfy his material wants. Epigraphical sources shows that donees had superior rights over peasantry. The donees were entitled to collect all kind of taxes. They were able to collect regular and irregular taxes and fixed and unfixed payment. The donees were empowered with the right to evict the peasantry at will and to replace them with new peasant. The land-grants charters edicted the peasants to carry out the orders of the donee as long as they were alive. It is argued that exorbitant taxes were imposed in the areas of a feudal chief with the result than often the peasant had even to sell their plough, plough shares, yokes and all other requisites of cultivation at times they were forced to sell their children. The largest segment of society in early medieval India was exploited and their economic condition worsened miserably. The popular belief about the existence of Ramarajya (*i.e.* a state offering to the people all happiness and no misery) in ancient India largely remained a myth. Even the land-charters ordained that the tenants shall render to the donee the offering of the customary taxes such as *bhāga bhoga* and *hiraṇya* etc. It assigned a subordinate status and the peasants required to work as per the whims of the landlords? The peasants under the donees were subjected to reckless servility, while the free peasant lost in status because of the imposition of several new taxes in early medieval period.

It belies the earlier concept of enjoying land-grants, and certain kinds of land had been donated to different and state officials in lieu of cash salary for their services to the state *i.e.* pasture or baren land and land lying in the outlying regions of the states. The purpose of these land-grants probably were manifold; the king might have sincerely desired to bring uncultivable land under cultivation; secondly by granting the land in the far flung areas where the presence of royal authority was felt very little. Thus the king wanted to exercise its hold and presence in remote areas where people were oblivious to central authority.

No doubt, the fashion of making land-grants in Indian history was as old as Brahmana and Buddhist literature, but it has been used in different perspectives in different periods. The epigraphical sources of early India's indicate significant changes in the relation of the donors and the donees and consequently its impact on the state economy it has been in vogue since 8th Century onwards, officials of the state were remunerated through land-grants, whereupon a new class of landlords was created who were not Brāhmaṇas.

Thus, we infer that the grant of lands and villages with inhabitants, house-sites, cultivated or uncultivated fields, gardens etc. to pertained to the services rendered by the different cadres to the king, who were Brāhmaṇa, monks, religious as well as educational institution, servant and officers of the state.

There was general scarcity of currency in early medieval Northern Indian history. The metallic currency was almost absent in most part of northern India between 8th century to 1000 A.D. because of the decline of trade, further the grants of land to high officials in lieu of cash payments did away with the need for coins. Moreover, there are evidences for barter and the use of cowries as medium of exchange in daily transactions. The growing sense of localism and self-sufficiency of villages is reflected in expressions such as, *grāmacāra* and *sthānacāra* all referring to village, local practices in contemporary purāṇic literature.

It thus becomes abundantly clear that early medieval Indian villages were based on a self-sufficient economy where production approximated to local requirements with little attempt of producing a surplus for trade or exchange. Surplus production would hardly benefited the peasant, since it would have led to a demand from the landlord for a larger share. The regrouping and reorganization of social relationship *vis-á-vis* urban social milieu and the rise of landed aristocracy but also to the occupational immobility of the artisan by making them integral part of the jajmāni system.

It resulted in fracturing of agricultural system. It hastened the mixing of the classes with the *Brāhmaṇa* and *Kśatriyas*, adopting agriculture as an occupation whereas, the same was forbidden by *Dharmaśāstra* prescribed for *vaiśyas* and *śūdras*. It also reflected a change in perception of the individual because even the 'twice born' failed to sustain life merely based on *yajñas*. Consequently new determiners were evolved to ensure a new definition for agrarian growth and economy.

Hence, the fashion of frequent war during early medieval periods were mainly responsible for destruction of the economic life of the people. However, archaeological and literary sources reflected that invaders often attempted to destroy the economy. This political fragmentation dislocated the economy of the state or nation. My endeavour, therefore, have been directed in fulfilling the obligation in this research.

BIBLIOGRAPHY

(A)

Bhandarkar, D.R. *Corpus Inscriptionum Indicarum*, Vol. III (Revised), Delhi, 1981. Ed. By B.C. Chhabra and G.S. Ghai.

Chaudhary, R.K. (ed.). *Selected Inscriptions of Bihar*, Patna, 1958.

Epigraphia Indica, Government of India, Publication, Calcutta and Delhi, various editions.

Fleet, J.F. *Corpus Inscriptionum Indicarum*, Vol. III, Varanasi, 1963.

Gadre, A.S. *Important Inscription of Baroda State*, Vol. I, Baroda, 1943.

Hira Lal. *Descriptive Lists of Inscriptions in the C.P. and Berar*, Nagpur, 1932.

Karambelkar, V.W. *Selected Inscriptions of Sanskrit*, Nagpur, 1959.

Majumdar, N.G. *Inscriptions of Bengal*, III, *The Narendra Research Society Bengal,* Rajshahi, 1929.

Mirashi, V.V. *Inscriptions of Kalachuri — Chedi Era. C.I.I.* Vol. IV, Ootacamund, 1955.

Nahar, P.C. *Jaina Inscriptions*, 3 Vols., Calcutta, 1918-29.

Pandey, R.B. (ed.). *Historical and Literacy Inscriptions*, Varanasi, 1962.

Plogat, S.R. (ed.). *Inscriptions of Haryana*, K.U., 1978.

Romesh, K.V. *Inscriptions of Western Gangas*, I.C.H.R., Delhi, 1983.

Sircar, D.C. *Select Inscriptions*, Vol. II, Delhi, 1983.

Sen, B.C. *Some Historical Aspects of the inscription*, Calcutta, 1942.

Thaplyal, K.K. *Inscriptions of The Maukharies, Later Guptas, Pushpabhutis and Vasovarman of Kanauj*, I.C.H.R., Delhi, 1985.

Vogel J.Ph. *Antiquities of Chamba State I*, Calcutta, 1911.

(B) NUMISMATIC

Altekar, A.S. *The Gupta Gold Coins in Bayana Hoard*, Bombay, 1954.

Nadjer, D. *Second Supplementary. Catalogue of Coins*, Vol. I, Calcutta, 1977.

Chakraberty, S. *Socio-Religious and Cultural Study of The Ancient Indian Coins*, Delhi, 1986.

Gardener, P. *A History of Ancient Coinage* (700-300 B.C.) Oxford, 1975.

Gopal, L. *Early Medieval (Coins — Types of Northern India)*, Delhi, 1975.

Gupta, P.L. Coins, 4th ed., Delhi, 1996.

Hanola, D. *Studies in India Coins and Seals Delhi*, 1985.

Parkash, S. *Coinage in Ancient India*, Delhi, 1968.

Ray, P.C. *Coinage of Northern India*, Delhi, 1980.

Sharma, M.K. *Tribal Coins — A Study*, Delhi, 1944.

Singh, O.P. *Religion and Iconography on Early Indian Coins*, Varanasi, 1978.

Singh, R.U. *Coins of India*, Chandigarh.

Sircar, D.C. *Studies in Indian Coins*, Delhi.

Smith, V.A. *Catalogue of the Coins in Indian Museum*, Calcutta, 1906.

(C) ORIGINAL TEXTS IN INDIAN LANGUAGES AND THEIR TRANSLATION

Al-Biruni, Kitab-ul-Hind, (ed.) E.C. Sachau, 2 Volumes, London, 1910.

Amarashimha, Amarkoṣa, with Commentary of Ksīrasvamin and Vandyoghatiya-Sarvananda, (ed) T. Ganapati Sastri, Trivandrum, 1914-17.

Aitreyā Brāhmaṇa, (ed) A.B. Keith, (Rep.) Delhi, 1981.

Aparajita Prccha of Bhuvandeva, (ed) A. Mankad, Baroda, 1950.

Bāṇabhaṭṭa *Hanṣacharita* (tr) by E.B. Coroell and F.W. Thomas, London, 1909. *Harṣacharita of Bāṇa* (ed) J. Vidyasagra, Calcutta, 1892, *Kādambari*, (Tr) C.M. Ridding, London, 1896.

Bharvi, *Kirātarjunīyam*, with the commentary of Mollinatha, Calcutta, 1815 (ed) J. Vidyasagra, Calcutta, 1875.

Bhattanarayana, *Venisaṃhāra*, (Tr) S.M. Tagore, Calcutta, 1880.

Bhavabhuti, *Uttarāramacharita* (Tr) C.H. Tawney, Calcutta, 1871.

Bhoja, *Samaranganasūtradhara*, (ed) T. Ganapati Sastri, *GOS, XXV*, and XXXII. N.D. *Yuktikalpataru*, (ed) Isvara Chandera Sastri, Calcutta, 1917.

Bṛhaspati Smṛti (Tr) J. Jolly, *S.B.E.*, Oxford, 1889.

Buddhasuami, *Brhatkathaślokaśaṅgraha* (Tr) F. Lacote, 28 Vols., Paris, 1908-1929.

Chand Bardai, *Prthivirājarāso*, (ed) M.V. Pandia and Shamsunder Das, Banaras, 1913.

Damodara, Pandit, *Uktivyaktiprakaraṇa*, Bombay, 1953.

Dandin, *Daśakumāracharita*, (ed) G. Buhler, 1988-91; *Kāvyādarśa*, (Tr) S.K. Belvalka, Poona, 1924.

Devanabhatta, *Smṛti Chandrīkā*, (ed) L. Srimivasacharya, 6 Vols., Mysore, 1914-16.

Fonbes, A.K., *Rāsmālā* (ed) H.G. Rawlinson, Oxford, 1924.

Haribhadra, *Samaraichchakāhā* (ed) H. Jacobi, Calcutta, 1926.

Harisena, *Bṛhat-kathākośa*, (ed) A.N. Upadhye, Bombay, 1943.

Harivamsa (Tr) M.N. Dutta, Calcutta, 1897.

Hemachandra, *Abhidhānachintāmaṇi*, (ed) Hargovind Das Bechar Das and Muni Jinavijayji, Bhayanagar, 1914-1919. *Deśināmamālā*, (ed.) R. Pischel, P.V. Ramanujasuami, (2nd ed.) *BORI*, Poona, 1938. Kumārpālaeharita, Cantos, XXI-XXVIII, 2nd edition, *BORI*, Poona, 1936.

Jaimini, *Mimaṃsādarśana* with Sabara's commentary, (ed.) Maheśachandra, Calcutta, 1863-67.

Jātakas Stories (ed) E.B. Cowell, (Tr) Robert Chalmers, (rep.) Cambridge, 1973.

Jimutavahana, *Dāyabhāga* (Tr) H.T. Colebrooke, Calcutta, 1910.

Kṛṣi-Parāśara (ed.) G.P. Majumdar and S.C. Banerji, Calcutta, 1960.

Kṣemendra, *Bṛhatkathāmañjari* (ed.) Sivadatta and Parab, Bombay, 1931.

Kṣemendra, *Deśopadeśa* (ed.) M. Kaul, Poona, 1938.

Panchatantra (ed) W.F.F. Edgerton Text — with translation, Poona, 1924.

Purāṇa Agni (Tr) M.N. Dutt, 2 vols. Calcutta, 1903-4.

Purāṇa Brāhma, Poona, 1895.

Purāṇa Devī (Tr) Vijnananda; Allahabad-N.D.

Purāṇa Kālika, Venkatesvara Press, Bombay, 1829.

Rājaśekhaka, Bālarāmayaṇa (ed.) Govinddeva Sastri, Banaras, 1869.

Rgvedasamḥita (Tr) H.H. Wilson, 7 Vols., Delhi, 1977.

Kavyamimamsa (ed.) C.D. Dalal and R.A. Sastri, Baroda, 1934.

Karpauramañjari (tr) C.R. Lanman, Cambridge, 1901.

Manu *Manusmṛti* with Kullukabhatta's Commentary with Medhatithi's commentary (ed) Ganganatha Jha, Calcutta, 1932.

Mahābhārta (Tr) P.C. Roy, Calcutta, NDs Tr K.M. Ganguli, Various Vols., Delhi, 1975.

Marcopolo, *The Travels of Marcopolo* (Tr) A. Rioci, (3rd ed.), London, 1950.

Mitramisra, *Paribhāsāprakōśā* part of *Viramitrodaya*, Banaras, 1906.

Motichandra, *Sārthvaha*, Patna, 1953.

Sandhya Kananandi, *Rāmacharita*, (ed.) R.C. Majumdar, R.G. Basak and N.G. Banerji, Rajshahi, 1939.

Somadeva, *Kathāsaritsāgara* (ed.) C.H. Tawney, (ed) By Penzer as the ocean of story, London, 1924-28.

Somasvara, *Mānasollāsa* (ed.) G.K. Shrigondekar, 2 Vols., Baroda, 1928.

Jinesuara Suri, *Kathākośa*, (Tr) C.H. Tawney, London, 1895.

Kalhana, *Rājataranginị* (eds. — Tr.). M.A. Stein, Westminster, 1900.

Kātyayanasmṛti (Tr) P.V. Kane.

Naisadhiyacharitam of Śrīhari (Tr) K.K. Handique, Lahore, 1934.

Laksmidhara, *Krtyakalpataru* (ed.) with an introduction by K.V.

Rāmāyaṇa (ed) O.P. Shah, Oriental Institute, Borada, 7 Vols., 1962-75.

Rangswami in eleven volumes, of GOS, Baroda, 1944-1953.

Sadhuktikarṇamota of Śrīdharadasa (ed) R. Sharma, Lahore, 1933.

Sudraka *Mṛchchhakatika*, (ed) A.W. Ryder, Cambridge, 1905.

Śukra *Śukranitisāra* (Tr) By B.K. Sarkar, Allahabad, 1914.

Upamitibhavapropncakathā of Siddharsi, (ed) P. Peterson, Calcutta, 1899.

Varāhamihira, *Bṛhatsamhita* (Tr) S. Sastri and M. Ramakrsna, Bangalore, 1947.

Vijñneśvara, *Mitakṣara*, Bombay, 1926.

Yājnavalka, *Yajñavalkyasmṛti* (ed) J.R. Gharpure, Bombay, 1936.

(D) SECONDARY SOURCES

Abdul Rahman Samdesa—*Rāsaka*, V.S. 2001.

Agrawala, R.C. "Dramm in Ancient Indian Epigraphs and Literature".

Journal of the Numismatic Society of India, Vol. 17, 2, pp. 64-82, 1955.

Agrawala, V.S. *Harshacharita — Ek Sānskritik Adhyayan*, Patna, 1953.

———. *Kadambari-Ek-Sānskritik Adhyayan, Varanasi*, 1958.

Ahmad, Nizam-ud-dn, *Tabaqat-I-Nasiri* (Tr) B. De, 3 Vols., Calcutta, 1913-14.

Aiyangar, K.V.R. *Aspects of Ancient Indian Economic Thoughts*, Baranas, 1934.

Al-Sharif Al-Idrisi, *Kitab nuzhat Al-Mushtaq Fi Khiraq Al Afaq* (*India and the Neighbouring Territories*) Tr. S. Maqbul Ahmad, Leiden, 1960.

Altekar, A.S. *Raṣtraliṭas and Their Times*, Poona, 1934.

———. *State and Government in Ancient India*, Banaras, 1949.

Anderson, P. *Lineages of the Absolutist State*, London, 1979.

———. *Passage from Antiquity to Feudalism*, London, 1936.

Asopa, J.N. *Feudalism in North India* (700-1200 A.D.), Jaipur, 1989.

———. *Origin of the Rajputs,* Delhi, 1976.

Avenere, S. *Karl Marx on Colonialism and Modernization*, New York, 1969.

Awasthi, A.B.C. *History from the Purāṇa*, Lucknow, 1975.

Baily, A.M. & Joseph, *The Asiatic Mode of Production Science and Politics*, London, 1981.

Baden Powell, *The Indian Village Community,* London, 1908.

Bagchi, P.C. *India and China* (2nd ed) Bombay, 1950.

Bandopadhyaya, N.C. *Economic Life and Progress in Ancient India Vol. I* (2nd ed) Calcutta, 1945.

Barua, B.K. *A Cultural History of Assam, Nowgong*, 1951.

Basham, A.L. *The wonder that was India*, 1953.

Beteille, Andre, *Studies in Agrarian Social Order,* Delhi, 1974.

Beal, S. *Si-yu-ki: Buddhist Records of the Western World,* 2 Vols. London, 1884.

Bhatia, *The Paramāras* (800-1305), Delhi, 1970.

Bhattacharya, N.N. *Ancient Indian Ritual and Their Social Content*, Delhi, 1975.

Bhargava, B. *Indigenous Banking in Ancient and Medieval India*, Bombay, 1934.

Bloeh, M. *Feudal Society,* 2 Vols. (Fr) by L.A. Manyon, London, 1965.

———. *Land and Work in Medieval Europe*, London, 1967.

———. *Slavery and Serfdom in the Middle Age* (Tr) W.R. Beer, London, 1975.

Bois, G. *The Crises of Feudalism*, Cambridge, 1984.

Bose, N.S. *History of Candellas,* Calcutta, 1956.

Bose, P. *The Hindu Colony of Cambodia*, Adyar, 1927.

Briggs, John. *The Peasant Land Tax in India*, London, 1830.

Burns, J.F. *Middle Ages*, New York, 1946.

Burgess, J. *Archaeological Antiquities of Northern Gujrat*, London, 1903.

Byres, T.J. and H. Mukhia (eds). *Feudalism and Non-European Societies*.

Special Issue of the Journal of Peasant Studies, Vol. 12, Non 2-3, London, 1985.

Chanana, D.R. *Slavery in Ancient India*, Delhi, 1960.

———. "Ideological Aspects of Slavery in Ancient India" *J.O.I.*, VIII, Delhi, 1959.

Channa, Subhadra. "Indian Peasantry : Some Analytical Issues", in V.K. Thakur & A. Aounshuman (eds) *Peasant in Indian History I,* Patna, 1996.

Chanslra, B. *Karl Marx His Theories of Asian Society and Colonial Rule*, Delhi, 1981.

Chakraborti, D.K. *The Early use of Iron in India*, Delhi, 1992.

———. *Ancient Indian Cities*, Delhi, 1995.

———. "Distribution of Iron ores and the Archaeological Evidence of Early Iron in India" *JESHO*, Vol. XX, Pt. 11, Leiden, 1977.

Chakrabarti, N.P. *India and Central Asia*, Calcutta, 1927.

Chatterji, B.R. *India and Java*, Calcutta, 1933.

Chaudhary, R.K. "Feudalism in Ancient India", *J.I.H.*, Vol. 37, 38.

———. "Problem and Methods of Socio-Economic History of Ancient India in a New Perspective", *JBRS*, Vol. 54, Patna, 1968.

———. "Some Aspects of Feudalism in Cambodia". *JBRS*, Vol., 47.

———. "Visti (Forced Labour) In Ancient India", *IHQ*, 1962.

———. "Some Historical Aspects of Feudalism in Ancient India Down to the 14th Century A.D. Based mainly on the Epigraphic Source," *JIH*, Vol. 38, pts 1-3, 1960.

———. "Peasants in Ancient India", *J.B.R.S.*, Vol. LIX, pts 1-4.

Chaudhury, P.C. *The History of Civilization of the People of Assam upto the 12th Century A.D.*, Gauhati, 1959.

Chakravarti, Uma, *The Social Dimensions of Early Buddhism*, Delhi, 1987.

Chattopadhyaya, B.D. *The Making of Early Medieval India*, Delhi, 1994.

———. "Origin of the Rajputs: The Political, Economic and Social Processes in Early Medieval Rajasthan," *IHR,* Vol. 3, 1976.

———. *Aspects of Rural Settlements and Rural Society in Early Medieval India*, Calcutta, 1990.

———. "Markets and Merchants in Early Medieval Rajasthan", *Social Science Probings*, Vol. 2.4. 1985.

———. "Irrigation in Early Medieval Rajasthan" *JESHO*, Vol. 16, pts. 2-3, 1973.

———. "Trade and Urban Centres Early Medieval North India", *IHR*, Vol. 1,2, 1974.

——— (ed). *Essays in Ancient Indian Economic History,* Delhi, 1987.

Chauhan, G.C. "Sāmanta as a Feudal Lord in Early India", *JOI*, Vol. 39, No. 1-2, Pune, 1989.

———. "The Aśvamedha as the symbol of one's overlordship", *QRHS*, Vol. XXXII No. 1-2, Calcutta, 1991.

———. The Traces of Feudal Culture as Reflected in two *Praśastis* of Baijnāth", *M.D.U.R.J.,* Vol. 6, No. 1, Rohtak, 1991.

———. "Feudalisation of Educational Institutions in Early India", *JOI*, Vol. 43, Nos. 1-2, Baroda, 1993.

———. "Feudal System of Balson and Baijnāth States in H.C.V., Shimla, 1996.

———. "Traces of Feudalism as Reflected in Copper-plate Inscription of Nirmaṇḍ", *ABORI,* Vol. 31, Pune, 1996.

———. "The Artisan: A Question of Socio-Economic Contrast", *JOI*, Vol. XLVI, No. 3-4, Baroda, 1997.

———. "Slave Mode of Production in Early India", *QRHS*, Calcutta, 2000.

———. *Origin and Growth of Feudalism in Early India* (from The Mauryas to 650 A.D.), Delhi, 2002.

Commissariat, M.S. *History of Gujrat*, London, 1926.

Coulbourn, R. (ed). *Feudalism in History*, London, 1956.

Cox, T. "Awkward Class or Awkward Classes, Class Relation in the Russian Peasantry before Collectivisation" *Journal of Peasant Study*, London, 1979.

Critchleg, J. *Feudalism*, London, 1978.

Dange, S.A. *India from Primitive Communism to Slavery*, Bombay, 1949.

Das, S.K. *Economic History of Ancient India*, Calcutta, 1926.

Datta, Swati, *Migrant Brāhmaṇ in Northern India*, Delhi, 1989.

Datta, B.N. *Dialectives of Land Economic in India*, Calcutta, 1950.

Davahuti, D. *Harsha: A Political Study*, London, 1970.

Devi, S.M. *Economic Condition of Ancient India* (from A.D. 750 to 1200), Delhi, 1987.

Deyell John S. *Living without Silver, The Monetary History of Early Medieval North India*, Delhi, 1990.

Dietze, C. Von, "Peasantry" In *Encylopaedia of the Social Sciences*, (ed) E.R.R. Selgman, Toronto, 1950.

Elliot, H.M. and Dowson, J. *The History of India as told by its own Historians*, 8 Volumes, London, 1866-67.

Elphinston, M. *The History of India*, Leiden, 1905.

Erdosy, G. *Urbanization in Early Historic India*, Oxford, 1988.

Farquin, G. *Lordship and Feudalism in the Middle Ages*, London, 1976.

Firykenberg, R.E. (ed). *Land Control and Social Structure in Indian History*, Delhi, 1969.

Ganguly, D.C. *History of Paramara Dynasty*, Dacca, 1933.

Ganguly, B.N. "The Indian Peasant as an Analytical Category", Sociological papers, *XIIth All India Sociological Conference*, Varanasi, 1974.

Ghoshal, U.N. *Contribution to the History of Hindu Revenue System*, Calcutta, 1929.

———. *The Agrarian System in Ancient India*, 1930.

———. *A History of Indian Political Ideas*, Oxford, 1959.

Gopal, K.K. "Feudal Composition of Army in Early Medieval India", *Journal of the Andhra Historical Research Society*, Vol. 28, pts. 3-4, 1962-63.

———. "Assignments to Officials and Royal Kinsmen in Early Medieval India (700-1200 AD)", *University of Allahabad Studies*, 1963-64.

———. "The Assembly of the Samantas in Early Medieval India", *JIH*, Vol. 42, pt. 1, 1964.

Gopal, L. "Sāmanta — Its Varying Significance in Ancient India", *J.R.A.S.G.B.I.,* 1963.

———. "Coins in the Epigraphical Literary records of Northern India in the Early Medieval Period", *Journal of the Numismatic Society of India*, Vol. 25, pt. 1, 1963.

———. "On Feudal Polity in Ancient India", *JIH*, Vol. 41, 2.

———. "Quasi-Manorial Rights in Ancient India", *JESHO,* Vol. 6, Leiden, 1963.

——. *The Economic Life of Northern India C.A.D.* 700-1200 (2nd ed), Delhi, 1989.

———. *Aspect of the History Agriculture in Ancient India*, Varanasi, 1980.

Goyal, S.R. *Harsha and Buddhism*, Meerut, 1986.

Gupta, A.D. *A History of Indian Economic Thought*, London, 1993.

Habib, I. "The Peasant in Indian History," *General President's Address, IHC*, 43rd, Session, Kurukshetra, 1982.

——— (ed). *Interpreting Indian History*, Shillong, 1985.

Habib, M. *Sultan of Mahmud of Ghazni*, Aligarh, 1927.

Hazra, R.C. *Studies in the Upapurāṇa*, Vol. I, Calcutta, 1958.

Henige, D.P. "Some Phantom Dynasties of Early and Medieval India: Epigraphic Evidence and the Abhorrence of Vacuum",

Bulletin of the School of Oriental and African Studies, Vol. 38.3, 1975.

Herlipy, D. *The History of Feudalism*, New York, 1976.

Hourani, G.F. *Arab Seafaring in the Indian Ocean in Ancient and Early Medieval Times*, Princeton, 1951.

I-tsing. *A Record of the Buddhist Religion as Practised in India and the Malaya*, Archipelago, (Tr. E) Takukusu, Oxford, 1896.

Inden, R. "Hierarchies of Kings in Early Medieval India", *Contribution to the India Sociology*, Vol. 15, 1981.

Jha, D.N. *Revenue System in Post-Mauryan and Gupta Times*, Calcutta, 1967.

———. "Early Indian Feudalism : A Historiographical Critique", *Presidential Address*. *PIHC*, 40th session, Waltair, 1979.

———. Studies in *Early Indian Economic History*, Delhi, 1980.

——— (ed). *Feudal Social Formation in Early India*, Delhi, 1987.

———. *Economy and Society in Early India : Issues and Paradigms,* Delhi, 1992.

Jha, V. "Status of the Rathakar's Early *Indian History*", *PIHC*, 34th Session, Chandigarh, 1973.

———. "Position and Status of Bamboo-workers and Basket-Makers in Ancient and Early Medieval Times", *PIHC*, 39th Session, Hyderabad, 1978.

———. "Leather Workers in Ancient and Early Medieval India", *PIHC,* 40th Session, Waltair, 1979.

Jones, B. (Tr). *Feudal Society and Its Culture*, Moscow, 1988.

Karchroo, Vijay. *Ancient India*, Delhi, 2000.

Kaw, R.K. *Agriculture in Ancient India, ICAR*, Delhi, 1964.

Kosambi, D.D. *An Introduction to the Study of Indian History*, Bombay, 1956.

———. "On the Development of Feudalism in India, *ABORI*, Vol. 36 pt 3-4, Pune, 1956.

———. "Origins of Feudalism in Kashmir", *JBBRAS*, The Sardhasatabdi Commemoration Volume, 1956-57.

———. "Indian Feudal Trade Charter", *JESHO*, Vol. 2, 1959.

Krader, L. *The Asiatic Mode of Production*, Netherland, 1975.

Kula, W. *A Economic Theory of the Feudal System*, London, 1976.

Kulke, H.D. Rothermund, *A History of India*, (Rep.) New York, 1998.

———. "Fragmentation and Segmentation versus Integration? Reflections on the Concept of Indian Feudalism and Segmentary State in Indian History", *Studies in History*, Vol. 4, No. 2, Delhi, 1982.

Lahiri, N. "Landholding and Peasantry in the Brahmaputra Valley, C 5th-13th Centuries A.D., *J.E.S.H.O.*, Vol. 33, Leiden, 1990.

Larenzo, A.M. *Agricultural Labour Condition in Northern India*, Bombay, N.D.

Lamottee, E. *History of Indian Buddhism*, Louvain, 1988.

Maity, S.K. *The Economic Life of Northern India in Gupta Period* (300 to 500 A.D.), Calcutta, 1957.

Majumdar, A.K. *Chaulukyas of Gujrat*, Bombay, 1957.

Majumdar, B.K. *The Military System of Ancient India*, Calcutta, 1960.

Majumdar, R.D. *Ancient Indian Colonies in Far East*, 2 Vols., Dacca, 1937.

———. *Corporate Life in Ancient India*, Calcutta, 1927.

———. *Hindu Colonies in Far-East*, Calcutta, 1944.

———. *The History of Bengal*, Vol. I, Dacca, 1943.

Mazumdar, B.P. *Socio-Economic History of Northern India* (1030-1194 A.D.), Calcutta, 1960.

———. "Merchant and Landed Aristocracy in the Feudal Economy of Northern India (8th to 12th Century A.D.)" in D.C. Sarcar (ed) *Land System and Feudalism in Ancient India*, Calcutta, 1966.

———. "Epigraphic Records of Migrant Brahmana in North India", II, *IHR*, Vol. V, No. 1-2.

———. Industries and Internal Trade in Early Medieval North India", *Journal of Bihar Research Society*, Vol. 45-46, Patna, 1979-80.

Moreland, W.H. *The Agrarian System of Moslem India*, Cambridge, 1929.

Mukherjee, R. *The Foundations of Indian Economics*, London, 1916.

———. *The Rural Economy of India*, London, 1927.

———. *A History of Indian Shipping and Maritime Activity*, London, 1912.

Mukhia, H. "Was there Feudalism in Indian History", *The Journal of Peasant Studies*, Vol. 12, Nos. 2-3, London, 1981.

Nandi, R.N. "Growth of Rural Economy in Early India", *PIHC*, 45th Session Annamalai, 1984.

———. "Clint, Ritual and Conflict in Early Brahmanical Order, *IHR,* Vol. 6, 1979-80.

Nath, P. *Economic Condition of Ancient India*, London, 1929.

Niyogi, Pushpa, *Contributions to the Economic History of Northern India*, Calcutta, 1967.

North, D.C. "The Rise and Fall of Manorial System — A Theoretical Model", *IES XXXI*, 1971.

Ojha, A.P. "Blacksmiths in Ancient and Early Medieval India", *PIHC*, 40th Session, Waltair, 1979.

O'Learly, B. *The Asiatic Mode of Production: Oriental Despotism, Historical Materialism and Indian History*, London, 1989.

Parkesh, B. "The Genesis and Character of Landed Aristocracy in Ancient India", *JESHO*, Vol. XIV, Leiden, 1971.

Parsad, B. *The State in Ancient India*, Allahabad, 1974.

Prakash, Om. *Early Indian Land Grants and State Economy* Allahabad, 1988.

Pirenne, H. *Economic and Social History of Medieval Europe*, London, 1939.

Piggott, Stuart, *Pre-Historic India*, London, 1950.

Rai, G.K. "Forced Labour in Ancient and Medieval India", *IHR*, Vol. 3.1, Delhi, 1976.

———. *Involuntary Labour in Ancient India*, Allahabad, 1981.

Raychaudhri, S.P. "Agriculture in Ancient India" Dacca Uni. Studies, "A Short Account of Agricultural Methods and Practised in Ancient India", *Science and Culture*, Vol. 7, 1941.

———. "Agricultural Practices in India," *ICAR,* Review Series No. 4, 1953.

Ray, N.R. "The Medieval Factor in Indian History", *General President Address, PIHC*, 29th Session Patiala, 1967.

Ray, J.C. *Life in Ancient India*, Calcutta, 1948.

Randhawa, M.S. *A History of Agriculture in India*, Vol. I, Delhi, 1955.

Rangaswami, K.V. *Aspect of Ancient Indian Economic Thought*, Benaras, 1934.

Redfield Robert, *Peasant Society and Culture : An Anthropological Approach to Civilization,* Chicago, 1956.

Round, J.H. *Feudal England,* London, 1964.

Roslawlev, U., *The Agrarian Crisis in India*, Moscow, 1932.

Roy, B.P. *Historical and Culture Studies in the Puranas*, Allahabad, 1978.

Sachar, E.C. (ed). *Kitab-ul-Hind*, Vol. I, London, 1910.

Sharma, D.R. *Early Chauhan Dynasties*, Delhi, 1959.

———. *Rajasthan Through the Ages*, Bikaner, 1958.

Sharma, R.S. *Indian Feudalism*, Calcutta, 1965; 2nd (ed), Delhi, 1980.

———. *Light on Early Indian Society and Economy*, Bombay, 1966.

———. *Perspectives in Social and Economic History of Early India*, Delhi, 1983.

———. *Material Culture and Social Formations in Ancient India*, Delhi, 1993.

———. *Urban Decay in India* (circa 300 to 1000), Delhi, 1987.

———. *Land Revenue in India : Historical Studies*, Delhi, 1970.

———. "Feudal Elements in Raṣtrakuṭa Polity", *J.B.R.S.*, Vol. XLVI, 1960.

———. "Land Rents and Early Indian Economic History", in B.N. Ganguli (ed) *Reading in Economic History*, Bombay, 1965.

———. "Early Indian Feudalism (C 400-1200)" in S. Gopal and R. Thapar (eds) *Historical Writing in India*, Delhi, 1963.

———. "Feudal Elements in Pala and Pratihara Polity", *Studies in Asian History* (ed) K.S. Lal, Delhi, 1969.

———. "The Kali-Age : A Period of Social Crises", in S.N. Mukherjee (ed.) *Indian History and Thoughts*, Calcutta, 1992.

———. "Origins of Feudalism in India (400-650)", *JESHO*, 1, Leiden, 1958.

———. "Land-Grants to Vassals and Officials in North India (C AD 1000-1200)", *JESHO*, Vol. IV, Leiden, 1961.

———. "Feudal Economy under Pala and Pratiharas," *Vishwabharati Quarterly*, XXXVIII, No. 2, 1963.

———. "Land Right in Early Medieval India (500-1200), *Proceeding of XXVI International Congress of Orientalists*, Delhi, 1964.

———. "Coins and Problems of Early India Economic History", *PIHC,* 30th Session, Bhagalpur, 1968.

———. "The Economic History of India upto A.D. 1200 : Trends and Prospects (Jointly with D.N. Jha)", *JESHO*, XVIII, pt. 1, Leiden, 1974.

———. "Indian Feudalism Retouched", *IHR*, Vol. 1 No. 2, Delhi, 1974.

———. "How Feudal was Indian Feudalism?" *JPS*, XII, Nos. 2-3, London, 1985.

Shanin (ed). *Peasants and Peasant Society*, Harmondsworth, 1971.

Singh, Y.B. *Social Life in Ancient India*, Delhi, 1985.

———. "Halika-Kara: Crystallisation of Practice into Tax", *PIHC*, 43rd Session, Kurukshetra, 1982.

Silverman, Sydel. "The Peasant Concept in Anthropology", *JPS*, Vol. 7, No. I, London, 1979.

Sircar, D.C. (ed). *Land System and Feudalism in Ancient India*, Calcutta, 1966.

———. *Landlordism and Tenancy in Ancient and Medieval India*, Lucknow, 1969.

———. *The Emperor and the Subordinate Rulers,* Santiniketan, 1982.

Srimali, K.M. "Early Indian Coins and Economic History" in D. Handa (ed). *Ajaya Sri*, Vol. I, Delhi, 1989.

Srinivas, M.N. & A.M. Shah, "The myth of the Self-Sufficiency of the Indian Village", *The Economic Weekly* No. 12.

Tarafdar, M.R. "Trade and Society in Early Medieval Bengal", *IHR*, Vol 4.2, Delhi, 1978.

Thaper, Romila, *Ancient Indian Social History — Some Interpretation*, Delhi, 1978.

———. *From Lineage to State*, Delhi, 1984.

———. Bhattachary (ed). *Situating India History*, Delhi, 1986.

———. *History of India,* Vol. I, Delhi, 1968.

Thakur, Upandra. "A Study in Barter Exchange in Ancient India", *JESHO*, Vol. XV, Leiden, 1972.

Thakur, V.K. *Urbanisation in Ancient India*, Delhi, 1981.

———. *Historiography of Indian Feudalism; Towards a Model of Early Medieval Economy* (CAD. 600-1000), Patna, 1989.

A. Aounshuman (ed). *Peasants in Indian History*, I, Patna, 1996.

Thatcher (ed). *The Universal World Reference Enclyclopaedia*, Chicago, 1962.

Thorner, Daniel. "Peasantry" in D.L. Sills (ed) *International Encyclopedia of Social Sciences*, Vol. II, New York, 1950.

Trevaskis, H.K. *An Economic History of Panjab from Earliest Time to* 1890 (2nd ed), Gurgaon, 1989.

Vinogradoft, Paul. *Cambridge Medieval History*, Vol. II, London, N.D.

Yadava, B.N.S. "Secular Land-grants of the post-Gupta period and some aspects of the Growth of Feudal Complex in Northern India", in D.C. Sircar (ed) *Land-system and Feudalism in Ancient India*, Calcutta, 1966.

———. *Society and Culture in Northern India in the Twelfth Century*, Allahabad, 1973.

———. "Immobility and Subjection of Indian Peasantry in Early Medieval Complex", *IHR*, Vol. I, No. 1, Delhi, 1974.

———. "Problem of Interaction between Socio-Economic Classes in Early Medieval Complex", *IHR*, Vol. 3.1, 1976.

———. "The Accounts of the Kali Age and the Social Transition from Antiquity to the Middle Ages," *IHR*, Vol. 5, No. 1-2, 1979.

———. "The Problem of the Emergence of Feudal Relations in Early India", *PIHC*, Presidential Address, 41st Session, Bombay, 1980.

Watt, Sir, G. *Dictionary of Economic Products of India*, London, 1981.

Watters, T. *On Yuan Chwang's Travels in India*, 2 Vols., London, 1904-05, and (Rep. 1973).

Wiser, W.H. *The Hindu Jagmāni System*, Lucknow, 1936.

Williams, Raymond. Keywords, Georgow, 1976.

Williams, Sun M.M. *A Sanskrit-English Dictionary*, Oxford, 1960.

Williams, S.J. "Agriculture" in Chamber's *Encyclopaedia*, Vol. I, London, 1950.

JOURNALS

Journals of American Oriental Society.

Journals of the Andhra Historical Research Society.

Journals of Asiatic Society of Bengal, Calcutta.

Journal of the Asian and African Studies, London.

Journal of Bihar and Orissa Research Society, Patna.

Journal of Bombay Branch of Royal Asiatic Society, Bombay.

Journal of Bihar Research Society, Patna.

Journals of Bhandarker Oriental Research Institute, Pune.
Journal of the Economic and Social History of the Orient, Leiden.
Journal of the Economic History, Wilmington.
Indian Economic and Social History Review, Delhi.
The Indian Historical Review, Delhi.
Indian Historical Quarterly, Calcutta.
Journal of Indian History.
Journal of the Numismatic Society of India, Varanasi.
Journal of the Oriental Research, Madras.
Journal of the U.P. Historical Society, Lucknow.
Journal of Peasant Study, London.
Journal of Royal Asiatic Society of Great Britain and Ireland, London.
Journal of the World History (U.N.E.S.C.O.).
Proceeding of Indian History Congress.

Index